# Pulling Punches

# Pulling Punches

A TRADITIONAL FARMING YEAR

Paul Heiney

*With drawings by Tim Fargher*

Farming Press

First published in Great Britain 1988
Paperback edition 1994

Copyright © Paul Heiney 1988 & 1994

The moral right of the author has been asserted

Drawings copyright © Tim Fargher 1988 & 1994

ISBN 0-85236 283 8

A catalogue record for this book is available from the
British Library

Cover design by Andrew Thistlethwaite
Typeset by Galleon Photosetting, Ipswich
Printed and bound in Great Britain by
Biddles Ltd, Guildford and King's Lynn

*Dedicated to the Suffolk Horse*

# Preface to the Second Edition

ALTHOUGH it is a mere seven years since I strolled up to Weylands Farm one January morning to start my year as a farmer's boy, a lot of feet have plodded down many furrows since then, much water has flowed under the bridge, many sheaves of corn have gone through the binder.

The experience of working with Roger and Cheryl Clark, and their horses, left a deep impression upon me. Working the land had somehow infiltrated into the very depths of my soul and it was not long before I was hatching a plot to acquire a small farm of my own and carry on where this book leaves off. I have been farming, with Suffolk horses, in my own right for four years now and it has been the hardest years of my life. But I would not have missed it. Anyway, my year at Weylands Farm was such an intoxicating experience that it would have been impossible to turn my back on it and try to carry on as if it had been nothing out of the ordinary. I cannot thank the Clarks enough for the help and encouragement they gave me then, and have given me since, and I must also give thanks for the understanding and patience of my family on whom my farming project was somewhat thrust.

I have been lucky to share my own farming experiences with the readers of Saturday's *Times*, where I write my *Farmer's Diary*. The most commonly asked question is, 'Where did you start, how did it all begin?' The answer is here in this book.

PAUL HEINEY
*Middleton, Suffolk*
*July 1994*

# Preface to the First Edition

IN return for a very small favour that I had performed for the local vet, I was given an invitation to a dinner – the annual dinner of a society dedicated to the preservation of a rare breed of horse. In accepting, I did not realise that this modest ticket was going to provide me with the key to a world that was on the verge of extinction, and to a year of delight and discovery. It was a year packed with revelation, and with good honest toil of a kind it would be impossible to experience elsewhere.

As William Penn observed nearly three centuries ago, 'The country life is to be preferred, for there we see the works of God, but in cities little else but the works of men.' If I had been in any doubt about the abiding truth of that, it would have evaporated in twelve months so rich in a potent combination of work and fellowship that money could not have bought them: it has been a dream come true. In telling the tale, I have pulled no punches!

# Pulling Punches

# One

THE annual dinner of the Suffolk Horse Society brings together a strange mix of men. They come from all parts of Britain, but principally from East Anglia, and over a hot dinner pay homage to a breed of cart-horse: the Suffolk Punch.

Some will be remembering the horses as old friends with whom they spent countless hours in days that they recall as happier and more content than any since, but there will be arguments too. The question of which horse could plough the straightest furrow is as much chewed over today as when the disputed furrow was drawn, maybe fifty years ago. A man who achieved his reputation three score or more years back cannot rest in peace either, for, whether it is for the glories of his horsemanship or the stupidity of his ways that he is remembered, his name is sure to pass around the tables at the Annual Dinner.

'I remember that horse . . . why, that must have been nineteen thirty . . . er . . . six that must. I could have led him to that plough and he'd have done the job 'isself. That's true, that is,' an old boy boasted in his broad, sing-song Suffolk accent. He was horseman in charge of a dozen or more Suffolk Punches in the stables of one of the grand Suffolk estates. The sons of those estate owners were at the dinner too. They had their memories of the days when 4,000 acres was a decent parcel of land and

1

when a workforce of a hundred was a common thing. Now, sitting alongside the sons of the men their fathers dismissed when profits slumped and estates crumbled, they remembered the days when twenty horses to a farm was a commonplace. One son of a titled landowner said to me, wistfully, 'I can remember the day we burnt the cart-horse harness. It was the day the tractors came. I can remember it going on to the bonfire. And we were glad to see it go, then.'

On the table where I was sitting a few legends were being exhumed, like the one about the gallant Suffolk boy who walked to London. He was an apprentice farrier and had just forged a shoe that he thought was second to none. Not a single dent had the repeated blows of his hammer left on it: it was like a mirror. Seeking a wider stage on which to boast than that which the village forge could provide, he slipped the shoe in his pocket and walked to Crystal Palace, where his magnificent horse-shoe became the centre-piece of the Great Exhibition.

'That's true, that is,' said Roger Clark, a farmer who was sitting opposite me. He had just emerged from another long and involved tale with Hector, a farrier, who was sitting on my left. If I had understood the tale I would gladly re-tell it, but as the discussion became heated, so the accent grew thicker and I had to be content with understanding one word in ten. However, I did gather that the dispute centred around the way a horse had been shod and, 'That should never have been, that shouldn't!' I waited some time for a pause and got in quick with a question.

'When *was* all this?' I asked. They both looked up, silently. Quick sums were being done in their heads.

'Must have been about nineteen . . . twenty . . . five.'

2

And they both looked down at their plates and quietly tucked in. The long-running annual debate had been held and honour satisfied on all sides.

'What you've got to understand,' said Roger, 'is that there was no one prouder of his horses than a horseman on a farm. It didn't matter if they was going in the show-ring or coming back down the lane after a hard day's work, a horseman worthy of the name wanted his horses lookin' better than them next door.' At which point the chairman banged the table to call the room to order, and the engraved silver cups were awarded. Actually, Roger Clark was called to the rostrum to collect nearly all of them; for not only is he a farmer and farrier, he is also a highly respected and consistently successful exhibitor of Suffolk horses.

I could not make him out, to start with. His eyes fell easily into a distant stare, the stare of a man who is used to looking ahead as he follows a plough. Although he is only forty and could have little memory of the days when *only* the Suffolk horse tilled the Suffolk land, his working knowledge of horse-drawn cultivation seemed remarkably detailed. I knew he was an eminent farrier, a Fellow of the Worshipful Company of Farriers and reckoned to be at the very top of his profession ('I can tack a horseshoe on a fingernail, if I have to,' he once told a customer who thought a horse had got problem feet), but I sensed that there was more to him even than that, so I gathered up all my courage and quizzed his wife, who I had heard was a formidable lady.

Cheryl Clark is short in body but immense in strength and courage, and in will-power too. She first met Roger at the Woodbridge Horse Show twenty years ago and defied her father to marry him. She took up her husband's trade

3

and qualified as a farrier; she rides and hunts, but above all she breaks heavy horses to harness – no horse has ever broken her. She sports muscular arms that a grown man would be proud of. When the waitress meekly delivered a dish of chips intended to serve four, a sharp word from Cheryl had her scurrying back to the kitchen for more. That whole dish did for Cheryl. Her vocal range is impressive, both in the distance it can carry and the pitch to which it can rise. It is easy to see how one piercing word from Cheryl would crush the most truculent of animals.

She described her household. 'We've got six Suffolks at home in full-time work, and then we have others coming in for breaking. I've got two more Suffolks I'm breaking in and a couple of Shires, and I've got a couple of Percherons coming in before Christmas.' She spoke as if having in her charge six untamed horses, each weighing over a ton, was a matter of course.

'Naturally, we make our Suffolks work,' she announced.

I wasn't quite clear what she meant. She went on, 'They don't just stand around looking pretty. They have to work for their living.'

How?

'On the farm, of course,' she said, as if this was too obvious to be worth saying. 'We ain't got no tractors, just hosses!' If I'd had ears like a horse, they would have been pointing sharply forwards at this. I listened as she told me about the sowing and ploughing and the horse-drawn harvesting. She told me about the hundred-plus acres that they farmed as tenants on one of the large Suffolk estates; and about the mangel-wurzels and the kale and tares, the ducks and geese in the yard, the fattening pig in the sty.

'The horses plough the land, they pull the drill that

sows the seed and then they eat what they've grown. The horses eat the mangels, the sheep eat the tares.'

She might have been describing a family farm of the 1920s, or, I suppose, of any time up to the Second World War; not one that you would expect to flourish in Suffolk in the late 1980s. I know, because I live in Suffolk; in a farmhouse that would have been the beating heart of one of these small family farms, till the agricultural depression of the 1930s killed them off. These homesteads of a mere hundred acres or so were progressively swallowed by farmers richer than those who had been forced to leave the land, with the result that highly mechanised farms approaching a thousand acres are not uncommon now.

What dreary places many of them seem to be, adding little to the joy of the Suffolk landscape. Their unhedged fields provide little of the scenic light and shade that the old 'family farms' gave to the countryside. With this very much in mind, I listened carefully to what Cheryl Clark was saying about the way they farmed.

It became clear to me what set the Clarks apart from the rest. I resolved all the questions about them that were in my mind. They were not living in the past like so many other farmers at this dinner, who praised the glories of the Suffolk horse while back home the tractors rumbled relentlessly across their land. Nor were they self-appointed protectors of an endangered species, who might take an animal like a Suffolk horse and only parade it in public, never allowing it to fulfil its sole reason for being on earth, which is to work for its living. The Clarks have built their lives around their love of the Suffolk horse, and in return have given the horse what it needs most: land to plough and sow and reap. It is a circle of contentment.

I decided, across that dinner table, that I wanted to join

5

in. Not only to satisfy a journalist's curiosity about the working horse and this bygone slice of rural life, but because I too was brought up on farmyard stories of the speckledy-hen, Dobbin the carthorse, Daisy the milk-provider and tales of cross old Farmer Brown. For selfish, and undeniably romantic, reasons, at the age of thirty-eight, I wanted to be a farmer's boy.

# Two

*The sun had set beyond yon hill,*
*Across the dreary moor,*
*When weary and lame, a boy there came,*
*Up to a farmer's door;*
*'Can you tell me where ever I be,*
*One that will me employ,*
*To plough and sow and reap and mow*
*And be a farmer's boy, and be a farmer's boy?'*

I SET off one Sunday morning in late November, a
month after the dinner, with the intention of persuad-
ing the Clarks to take me on as a farm-hand and labourer,
one day a week for a year, so that I could grasp what
might be a last chance to learn to farm with horses. I had
no knowledge of agriculture and only a recent contact
with horses: light horses, of course, not 'heavies' like
Suffolks. But by the end of the year I wanted to be able to
call myself a horseman. More importantly, I wanted the
Clarks to think of me as a horseman as well. I wanted to
have followed the plough and the binder, and to have
reaped what I had sown.

The farm, 117 acres of south Suffolk, is a few miles
from a thundering trunk road. Cars heading north shoot
past Colchester, and first-time visitors nod in recognition

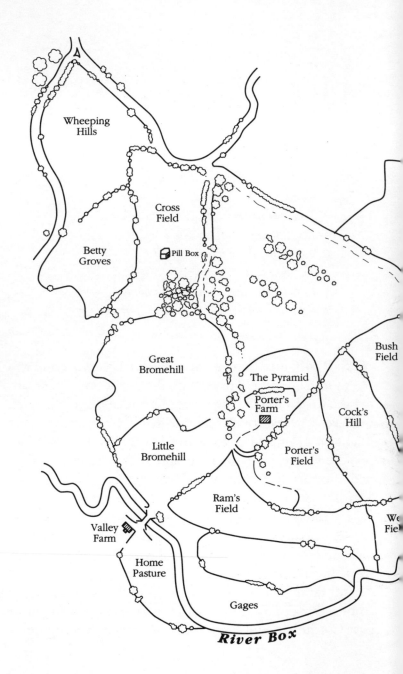

Wheeping
Hills

Cross
Field

Betty
Groves

Pill Box

Great
Bromehill

The Pyramid

Porter's
Farm

Bush
Field

Cock's
Hill

Little
Bromehill

Porter's
Field

Ram's
Field

We
Fiel

Valley
Farm

Home
Pasture

Gages

River Box

# Weylands
# Farm

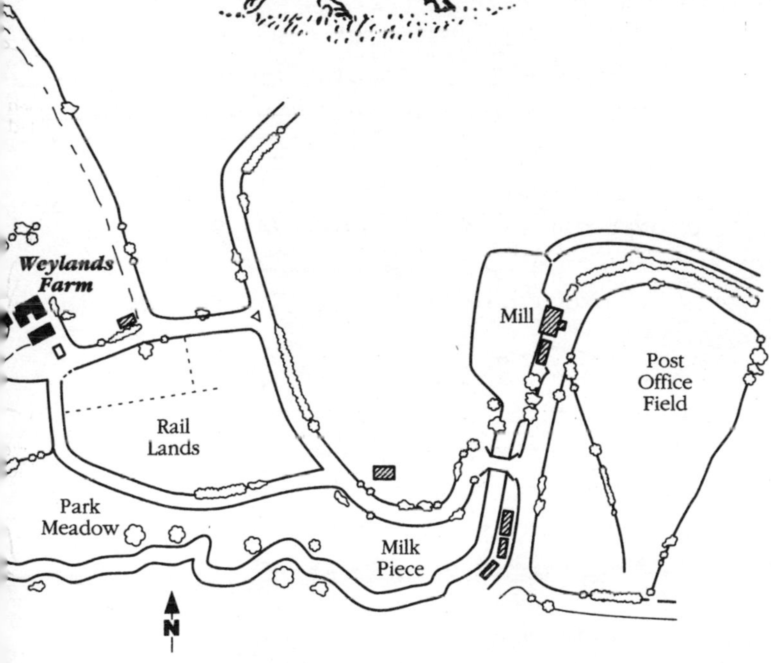

Weylands
Farm

Mill

Post
Office
Field

Rail
Lands

Park
Meadow

Milk
Piece

N

of the signs to Dedham and Flatford (Constable country) and then power on to Felixstowe or Great Yarmouth. They will probably never notice the turning to Stoke-by-Nayland. The road winds through Higham, and then, strangely for Suffolk, the land starts to rise steeply. Drive too quickly, and as you flash through the tiny village of Thorrington Street you will miss a sign that says simply 'By Road'. By implication it goes nowhere. In fact there can be few more interesting by-ways.

Drive over the narrow river Box and you climb more hills, following a lane that gets narrower between hedges that are even higher. And then there is the sign. I knew it was the place I was looking for by the large chestnut horse that was the painted centre-piece of it. I drove closer to read the peeling letters: 'R.J. & C.J. CLARK. SUFFOLK HORSES. WEYLANDS FARM.'

To the left, the land gently sloped till it met the river I had just crossed. A handful of sheep were grazing some hard patch of stubbly earth, working hard to get their teeth round the remnants of some greenery that was poking through the soil. A little further on was a muck-heap. Not a tip, or a dump, but a heap. Something that had been constructed rather than thrown together. It steamed.

No sight of a farmhouse yet, nor any horses. I stopped alongside the muck-heap to take in the view and the smell, both of which were impressive. Fields here were smaller than is usual on the large-scale farms of the 1980s, and handfuls of woodland had been left intact. Animals grazed. Not huge herds, but five or six cattle in one field, a couple of dozen sheep in another and a squealing crush of pigs in a filthy little midden of their own making tucked away in a corner. Some of the more distant fields

10

had been marked out with what looked like a single furrow made by one pass of a plough and left, as if a linesman had started to mark out a football pitch and run out of white paint.

The lane turned sharply to the right and the farmstead came out of hiding. It lies open only to the south, the least malicious of directions from which the winter wind can blow. For shelter, the house backs on to hills, so that although it might look from a distance as though it had been thoughtlessly perched on that hillside, it is in fact cosily cocooned on three sides.

It looks like a child's drawing of a farmhouse: white walls with a door in the middle and windows spaced symmetrically either side. The roof is of bright red pantiles with a brick chimney-stack slap in the middle of it, billowing black smoke. There is no path to the front door (there never is in East Anglian farmhouses: front doors are traditionally for weddings or funerals) so I went round the other side and found that the back door, with more yapping terriers standing guard than I could count, opened on to the farmyard itself. It had been a wet autumn, and so the yard was six inches deep in places with glutinous, boot-gripping mud. An arsenal of farm machinery was lined up: carts stood next to aged contraptions heavy with chains and cogs, which managed by their complexity to conceal what work they did. None had an engine. But still I saw no horses.

The back door opened and an overcoated, hunched figure stumbled out. His flat cap was well down over his forehead, and as he fumbled to deposit an empty beer bottle in the inner lining of his tired blue coat, it was impossible to guess if he was a fifty-year-old who had had a hard life, or an eighty-year-old who was doing well for

11

his age. He shuffled off in his wellington boots and I guessed he was probably a grand old gentleman of the land.

It was the middle of the day, dinner-time on the farm. Roger sat at the head of the table in the small kitchen, his back to an aged but serviceable coke-fired boiler. Bottles of horse medicine and veterinary books were littered around, and a shotgun was propped up in the corner. Doorsteps of toasted cheese were landing on the table with brisk regularity. The door to the sitting room was just ajar and I could see an array of silver trophies on a sideboard. Cheryl sat next to Roger, glued to the weekly farming programme on the television. A shiny twelve-wheeled harvester flashed across the screen, proudly showing its ability to crunch up so many acres of something or other per hour.

'Look what them wheels is doing to that land!' screamed Cheryl, voice instantly engaged in high gear. 'That land will be ruined, that will be. You wouldn't get horses' feet chewing up land like that.' She shook her head in disbelief. The commentator mentioned the many tens of thousands of pounds that this machine cost. Roger dropped his fork and leaned back in his chair.

'I could buy a fair few old hosses for that money,' and we laughed.

I explained my mission. I told them how I wanted to come and work here, one day a week for a year. Cheryl smiled.

'So, you want to come and work with us, do you?' She was enjoying every letter of the word 'work' as she twisted it around.

An advert flashed on the screen and caught her attention. It was for a multi-wheeled motorbike with fat pliable tyres for driving over rough and muddy ground. She drew in her breath as she watched it caterpillar across the countryside.

I asked where the horses were, the famous Clarks' Punches.

'Always turned out in the meadows on a Sunday. They work hard the rest of the week,' said Roger.

'I give 'em a bloody good physic on Sunday morning,' added Cheryl, and explained the laxative properties of a good bran mash and how it revitalised the jaded horses.

'I'll just join in and do any jobs that need doing with horses or anything else,' I said humbly, trying to steer the conversation back to my odd request. On the screen, the motorbike revved and screamed, flinging mud to either side as it careered around the countryside.

'That's rubbish what he says,' screamed Cheryl. I froze. She pointed at the screen. 'He says that that machine's the only thing that could get them places. A horse could.' God help the hapless salesman who turned up here trying to flog a tractor.

'Fridays and Mondays are the best days,' said Roger.

I begged his pardon.

'Fridays or Mondays are best if you want to come and work with us,' he repeated.

I realised I had got myself a job.

# Three

JANUARY the 2nd. Six-thirty in the morning, the sun not yet up, stars still clear in the sky. Despite a forecast of a mild day, Weylands Farm was a chilly place. There had been a frost, not strong enough to freeze the mud in the yard but sufficient to give a thin film of ice that crunched slightly underfoot. The first footfall broke through it, and I was soon up to the ankles in ooze; the second step I took more care over.

Sounds travelled great distances. Not sounds of engines or machinery here, but of contented munching. The barns where the horses were feeding were the noisiest. Anxious not to miss one grain of corn, the Suffolks stretched their broad necks and rattled their tethering chains along the edges of the mangers and licked long and hard into every corner. Then they moved on to the hay which had been stuffed into nets and hung within their reach, adding the sound of tearing as the horses' spade-like teeth ripped chunks of hay from the net. Then more loud munching.

There was no sign of human life. Six pigs watched anxiously from a corner of their electrically fenced mud hole, hoping for food. I was the only person around, so a dozen little piggy eyes followed my every move. Occasionally, their impatience would get the better of them and they would make a charge for the fence; there would be a blue spark as they collided with it, followed by a squeal, and when the echo of that had died away all would be quiet again. Except for the munching.

Out of the darkness came a young chap, heavily booted and sweatered. We exchanged a 'good morning' and he made straight for a lean-to at the end of the barn.

Then a piercing curse split the air. The day had begun. Cheryl was arguing with either a sack of corn or a leaking bucket. Her voice came from the deeper recesses of the big black barn from behind mounds of rolled oats and chaff and other grains. She came out of the shadows.

'I've been fighting. Good morning,' she said crisply.

She had, too, or she looked as though she had; and not with a sack of oats either. In the full light of the single bulb that lit the yard I could see her left eye; it was closed up, swollen and black. From her temples to her chin ran long grazes and bloody scratches as if she had been dragged sideways along a rough road. Perhaps the fight hadn't been a joke. I said nothing.

Smoke started to rise from a rusty chimney through the roof of the lean-to and, not being able to help Cheryl with her mixing and grinding, I set off to see what the smoke was all about. As I wandered through the barn, I heard a muttering and the occasional sound of steel prong hitting concrete, followed by the swish of straw being cast aside. It was the old boy, the 'grand old gentleman of the land', as I had thought of him. He was digging away with the fervour of a mole in the darker corners of the barn, a pitchfork in his hands and a good word for nothing on his lips. He didn't hear me, so I crept cautiously round the corner.

The smoke was coming from the forge, the heart of the farm where every day Roger Clark and his men shoe a

15

dozen horses. It is really two buildings in one. Two horses stand in one half, separated from each other by a baulk of timber that swings from the roof on two ropes; the other half houses the anvil, the fire, and the tools. Either side of the doorway stands a column of discarded horseshoes, enough to bring you a lifetime of luck. One pile I calculated to be a good ten feet high and four foot square, the other only a couple of feet off the ground. On this pile the old horseshoes were less rusty, but the heap was clearly growing daily. Within minutes of an air-blower being switched on, the coke at the centre of the fire was white-hot, and the smoke that didn't quite make it up the chimney was filling the forge and billowing into the still air outside. The lad I had met in the darkness coughed and looked at the clock. It was seven o'clock, and the first mechanical noise of the day could be heard chugging up the drive: the first paying customer, a hunting man, with his horsebox and horses to be shod.

The first day in a new job is always the hardest. I didn't know people's names, which building housed what, the difference between a ram and a ewe or a bucket of rolled oats and a bin full of bran. So I walked around some more. One room of the barn contained sacks piled high and a gas boiler hissing and rumbling in the corner. Sweet smells of boiled grain were carried along on the steam on this frosty morning. Chickens, scores of them, pecked and scavenged in every corner for precious ears of corn that had fallen from the scoops. Fine cockerels, with broad upright tail feathers of bright reds and oranges and white, strutted around in an imperious way while the hens just scuttled and pecked.

The 'old man' came round the corner with his pitchfork poised as if for the attack. His body was slightly bent and he shuffled along in his black wellington boots. His flat cap was pulled down across his eyes, the stuffing leaking from where the stitches round the peak had parted. If the jacket he was wearing had matched the trousers it would have made quite a smart suit; but as it was, the woollen trousers in grey herring-bone and the elderly shiny jacket in a brown tweedy tartan gave him the look of an eccentric gentleman of the road rather than of the land. The collar and tie didn't help; a little oasis of order amidst a confused jumble of clothing. He mumbled. I begged his pardon.

'Cold! Ain't it?' he grumbled, enunciating every syllable as if speaking to a half-wit, and rubbed his finger ends together before shuffling off with his pitchfork raised like an aged hunter still looking for a kill.

He hadn't gone many steps when a muffled shout from across the yard brought a flash of delight across his face. He put his fork down and as he made off towards the house his pace quickened. He mumbled something in his incomprehensible broad Suffolk accent. I begged his pardon. 'Break-fast,' he spelled out, and I followed him.

There is a wooden porch around the back door – a no-man's-land between the sludge of the farmyard and the cleanliness of the kitchen. It houses a few old lamb-feeding bottles, aged cardigans and sacks of potatoes. As I struggled there to release my feet from the clammy grip of my boots, I could hear raised voices around the kitchen table. The talk was of horses.

'Bad hosses should be shot!' I heard Cheryl declare, followed by a slam as she put down what sounded like a frying-pan.

'Sounds jolly severe,' said another haughtier voice. (This was the gentleman with the horsebox; favoured

17

early morning customers at the forge get a free breakfast thrown in.) I opened the wide and heavy wooden kitchen door and got the full force of Cheryl's argument.

'There's no point saying that hoss is a bad 'un' – she paused and looked at me – 'I've put everything on.' She had too; it was a fried breakfast of truly agricultural proportions – home-cured bacon, fried eggs, home-made sausages and doorsteps of fried bread. She went back to her argument. 'There's no point saying that hoss is a bad 'un, so we won't work her, we'll breed from her instead. That's bloody stupid, that is.' Her voice rose almost to cracking point.

'That's right, that is,' added Roger, who had been quietly tucking into his plateful. 'A good cart-horse needs no breaking, that don't,' he declared, and everyone around the table nodded in agreement as if at a harmonious board meeting.

From the tail end of the discussion, I tried to piece together the full story. It had started with Cheryl's black eye and scarred face. A couple of days before, she had been breaking two young Suffolk Punches to harness. It is a job that calls not only for skill, but endless patience and, when faced with a ton of young and untamed horse, no small amount of courage. Cheryl has a reputation for possessing more than enough of all these qualities.

The horses had been walking together down the lane, side by side, pulling Cheryl on a cart behind them. One of them, a twitchy, nervous youngster, had spotted something out of the corner of his eye that he didn't recognise and – assuming it to be foe rather than friend – had charged up a bank dragging the other horse with him. Cheryl was left behind on the road, having been tipped off the cart and dragged along the rough and stony ground still clinging to the reins. Hence the black eye and the hideous grazes down the face.

Some days before, the owner of the horse that had bolted had rung Cheryl up to ask how it was doing, only to be told that Cheryl thought the best thing for this horse was the bullet, given that it was 'daarft in the head' and likely to be a danger for the rest of its life.

'Bad hosses should be shot . . .' she declared, which was where I came in. It is apparently often suggested that if a horse isn't suitable for harness work, it might be used for breeding. If, like Cheryl, part of your living comes from teaching horses to behave and obey, the prospect of a strain of craziness and wilfulness being perpetuated is the last thing you wish to encourage. So the heartless argument in favour of the bullet and the knacker's yard starts to make sense.

The old man made quick work of his breakfast, picking up every inch of bacon rind, sucking off the last of the fat and throwing the rind to the dogs. I waited till he was out of earshot and asked Roger what he was called. His name was Gerald.

'Grand old boy,' I said, assuming it to be the right thing to say. Cheryl was now back, Gerald outside putting his boots on.

'Grand old boy be buggered,' she shrieked and all at the breakfast table rocked with laughter. Even the dogs joined in.

'That's fags and booze that done that,' Roger told me with great glee on his face.

'Now don't you believe one word he tells you,' added Cheryl, and the door opened and Gerald was back amongst us. I hoped, for the sake of my future working relationship with him, that he hadn't heard us.

19

Under his breath, he asked Roger what was to be done. Roger gazed through the window, put on his cap and after a good half minute's solid thought said, 'We'll do that bottom yard. Prince in the cart. Richard and Courtier turned out, and Rupert and Thomas to plough after dinner.' These, of course, were the horses and not the men. The only men on the farm, apart from Fred, the apprentice farrier, and Stuart, second-in-command in the forge, whom I had stumbled across earlier that morning, were me and Gerry – not much of a match for a hundred acres of land which can fight you every inch of the way, as I was to discover.

Roger stood up and strode towards the forge with the gait of a man who was going about his real business in life. He disappeared into the lean-to and within seconds the chimney was billowing again and the chime of hammer hitting anvil was ringing out. Back in the kitchen, Gerry was wringing out the dishcloth.

'We'll get them hosses sorted, then,' he said to me, and I followed him to the barn. Work was about to begin.

I counted only six brown, round bottoms in the stalls, although I was sure they said there were twelve horses on the farm. The stalls, or 'standings', are where the horses stand throughout the working day with their heads tethered by a short chain to the wall and within easy reach of a net bag stuffed with hay. (At night, they are free to wander in the yard in the traditional manner.) In front of their noses is a large wooden manger the size of a small water tank. This is for regular and copious supplies of a carefully balanced cocktail of corn, chaff and various other sweet-smelling and nutritious grains that keep these monster horses alive and working, but definitely not kicking.

Each horse is separated from his neighbour by a low wall, and along the back of the row of horses runs a narrow gangway down which you have to walk to get to the harness-room and the feed store. This means that you are spending much of your time within easy kicking distance of a dinner-plate-sized hind hoof. That might be a problem in a stable of highly strung racehorses, but the legs of these Suffolks stand with the impassive benevolence of oak trees. I soon felt confident enough to wander up and down the standings with only half an eye on them instead of my full attention. Perhaps I should get caught out one day, but for the moment I trusted them. I liked the look in their eyes, which was one of willingness and obedience. I liked the size of them, which strangely I did not find threatening. But most of all, on this chilly morning, I liked them for the heat which they threw out

21

as efficiently as any well-fired stove.

It was a dusty, cobwebby old building, with broken forks here and old horse-brushes there. Anything that was directly concerned with the horses' welfare, however, was of the high standard of a comfortable country hotel. Any horse-muck was forked away as quickly as it was dropped, and the straw on which they stood was not only frequently replaced so that it always looked fresh and golden, but it was plumped up with the pitchfork much as a chambermaid might give an eiderdown a good shaking. The hay smelt sweet, and if the rafters were strung together with a maze of cobwebs, this was a positive benefit: each would serve as a summer graveyard for the hordes of flies that would otherwise descend and make the horses' lives as uncomfortable as they could.

Lynn, a young girl from the nearby village, arrived. She was the stable groom and looked like a younger and less muscular version of Cheryl. She gave me a brush and told me to start at one end and work my way along. Did she mean one end of the horse or one end of the stalls? Either was a daunting prospect, like taking a paintbrush to restore the white cliffs of Dover. But it was cold, and the animals were warm to the touch, so it didn't take many strokes of the brush before I was hanging up my coat. By the time I had brushed from neck to tail I had worked up a sweat, and an affection. They were kindly animals. I'm not certain why I thought that, but they radiated not just warmth of body, but of spirit too. They would rub their heads on your shoulder in an affectionate way, and give an appreciative glance backwards as I brushed away the sweat and mud of the previous day's work.

But how was I ever going to recognise them and put names to them? They weren't all the same, by any means.

Some had much lighter manes, others had broader chests, some had their eyes closer together; but basically they were all big brown horses, so when Lynn or Gerry said 'Is Richard brushed?' I could only ask which was Richard and then forget as soon as I had been told.

Gerry was muttering. He was always muttering, and never a word could I understand. It was only when a muttering was repeated more loudly that I realised it was a question and so, 'You what, Gerry?' became my theme for the morning. I followed him into the harness-room. This was not the home of the show harness, the highly polished leather and burnished brasswork that parades round the show-rings and helps to win the silver cups. At least, I hoped it wasn't, for it would have taken an army of squaddies with boot-polish brushes to put a shine on any of this hard-worked leather. This was the day-to-day working harness which couples the horses to the carts or the ploughs, or to the other farm machinery, such as seed drills, harrows or cultivators.

Anyone used to 'ordinary' horses and the way they are harnessed would not feel much at home in this tack-room. The harness is, of course, much bigger. Two ponies could get their heads through one Suffolk's collar, and one man alone would find it quite a burden to lift if it were fitted with heavy wooden hames and chains. Prince, the horse nearest the door, bowed his head politely as, with a groan and a heave, I lifted the collar over his broad head and slid it down his neck. Gerry was rattling away behind me like Marley's ghost and I left the tangled chainwork to him. Last of all came the bridle and the rough iron bit – not at all like the smooth plated affairs that pamper the mouths of less heavy horses.

With the horse 'collared', we led Prince out into the

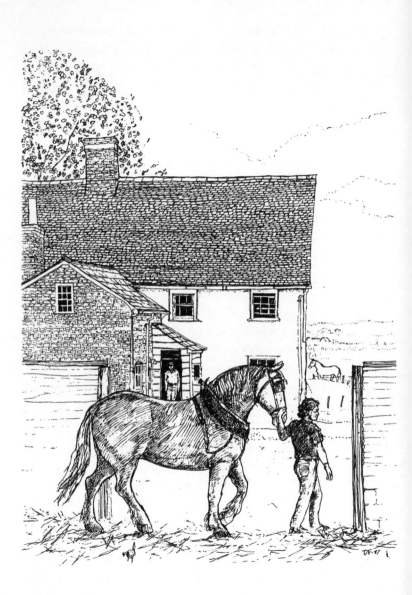

yard. This in itself was a feat since there was little turning space and, wearing the broad blinkers, Prince couldn't see behind him. So he shuffled foot after foot till he worked his head towards the door and then stumbled into the yard like an obedient dog. Gerry had hold of the leading rein but it was hardly necessary; Prince could have got there on his own.

The tumbril, or tip-cart, used for general carting work was waiting in the yard: another scene from a children's Farmyard Book. It was built of wood, and quite recently compared with other implements in the yard. The shafts between which Prince was to stand were pointing to the sky, and the back of the cart was resting on the ground. It had the previous owner's inscription on it, which gave a clue to its age: 's. JOHNSON. 1950.'

Gerry swung Prince round till he had his back to the cart, and then, with an effective combination of pulling and growling, 'Guuurt back hoss . . . guurrt over . . .' he placed the horse's broad rear-end between the shafts. Then we heaved on the cart till the shafts came down on either side of him and the rusty chain that linked them came to rest across the saddle on Prince's back. A couple more chains to hook on, and we might be in a position to start work. We had fed, and brushed, and harnessed, and hooked the horse into the cart. If it had been a race between us and a tractor-driver who had only to turn an ignition key, we would have been left standing in a cloud of exhaust smoke long ago. But we weren't. We were in fresh air that was getting colder by the minute. I could tell that from the steam puffing out of Prince's nose – and the dew drop on the end of Gerry's.

Still, you don't feel the cold when you're muck-carting, which was our job for the entire morning. It is work that makes you sweat, as you fling heavy forkfuls of rotting horse-muck high on to a growing pile that is already quite a distance up on a high cart. In addition, the muck itself keeps you warm. As any compost-making gardener will tell you, rotting vegetation gives off heat. Rotting dung, as provided in great quantities by the horses, gives it off even faster. I could feel the warmth spreading up through the soles of my rubber boots as we trampled across the muck that lay deep across the yard.

They have a system for dealing with it on Weylands Farm that, at first sight, appeared to be a lazy man's way of doing things; but I was beginning to appreciate that nothing on this farm was done without good reason. They just throw it out of the stable doors and let it lie on the yard. 'That's how we make *good* muck,' said Roger. 'You've got to have *good* muck. We just throw it down, spread it around a bit, the horses stand on it all night and break it down, they wet on it and then that's the start of *good* muck, that is. There's no point just shovelling it out of the stables and on to the muck heap, no point at all.'

Prince and his cart were backed into the yard and Gerry gave me a fork, jealously keeping the fork he always used. I couldn't see any difference between his and the one he gave me, but it seemed to make him happy. Prince stood perfectly still, as if his feet had been set in concrete, and we started to load up. The muck in the yard was deeper than it looked, a good foot in places, and the deeper you dug the denser it became; so the forkfuls became smaller and progress slower. You might be digging and suddenly hit a pocket of pungent gas which could set you reeling, but by and large there is nothing offensive about rotting horse-muck, even ten tons of it – roughly the amount we were expecting to move.

When you are not fit, when the muscles that raise your laden arms above your head have not had a strain like this placed upon them for as long as you can remember, you ache. You ache after the first cartful and you wince even more when Cheryl breezily walks past shouting with great mirth, 'I don't want to see them forks stop moving. Twelve loads per man per day, that's what they used to shift,' and with a broad grin she was off.

Whenever I suggested to Gerry that we had a full load, he would always insist on 'one more forkful, juss one more'. Even when it was teetering over the brim of the cart ready to fall back into the yard and I suggested it would be time to call it a load, back would echo that familiar 'one more forkful, juss one more'.

I tried to talk as we made repeated trips up the lane to the muck-heap near the farm entrance. It wasn't easy. Short replies I could understand, but long mumbled sentences I found difficult. 'How long have you worked with horses, Gerry?'

'Forty-five years. I hate tractors, hate 'em. That's not to say I can't drive 'em, 'cos I can. They say that there's no one as can drive a seed drill as straight as I can, but I don't like 'em, tractors, I don't,' and he wiped his nose on his sleeve. He looked up to the sky and gazed around while he caught his breath. 'That'll be rain settin' in later.' I longed to read the signs, the weather portents that Gerry had seen in the skies. But I knew that if I asked him what he had based his forecast on, I might not have been any the wiser. Anyway, shortly after, the sky cleared and it turned brighter for the rest of the day, so I was glad I didn't bother.

After the fourth ton, the job takes on a rhythm which is dictated by the horse and which to my surprise I found relaxing and in perfect harmony with the pace at which a man might be expected to work. A tractor driver might feel he is a slave to his machine; Prince and I were perfectly matched partners in this attack upon the yard and its six weeks' worth of muck. It works like this: it might take a hundred forkfuls to load the cart, after which you are gasping for breath. When you are about to fall on your knees, it is Prince's turn to work and he hauls the full load up the hill. By the time he is breathless and sweating, and you are once again refreshed and cooled by the gentle stroll, you unload the cart and Prince gets his breath back. Together you take the downhill route back to the yard and you are ready to start again. 'How many loads was that, how many?' asked Gerry. I didn't know and couldn't see the point in his question.

We carted a lot of muck in January. Even the snow didn't stop us. The snow came suddenly and ferociously on a Sunday night and blew on a strong north-easterly wind till drifts closed East Anglia for several days. No horses were shod on the farm that week, for no horses could get through. I remember the seven o'clock starts after a night of severe and penetrating frost which hung from every branch of every tree throughout the bitterly cold day. Even though the morning sun shone for many hours, the cold was so deep that the frosty silvering of the branches did not thaw one little bit. The landscape lost all its colour and the rich brown of the turned-out horses was visible for many miles.

The cold made the muck-carting even more pleasant, the warmth creeping through your boots a delight. The muck was heaped alongside various fields around the farm; and there it would stand, humming to itself, till after harvest-time, when it would be spread and ploughed in. It meant that some loads had to be carted up steep hills, so Prince and Richard went to the forge to have special studs called 'frost nails' hammered into their shoes – the equivalent of putting snowchains on a car. Roger claimed that with well-fitted frost nails, a horse could safely gallop over sheet ice.

To help haul a laden cart over the compacted and slippery snow and frost, the two horses were simply hooked one in front of the other; the leading horse being called the trace horse and the one that filled the shafts the shaft horse, filler horse or 'fill'us'. This outfit was a little more complicated to steer, especially when going round corners, so a loop of line was taken from either side of the bit of the trace horse and brought to the hand of whoever was driving. He then stood on the nearside of the two horses and halfway between them, so that he had the loop of cord in his left hand to steer the trace horse; while his right hand was free to steer the shaft horse by simply pulling on the leading rein.

It is a formidable place to stand, not only because of the sheer amount of horse that is towering above you (seven or eight feet at the head), but also because of the vastness of the feet which are pounding the ground only inches away from yours. If either of us misjudged a footfall, I pondered, it would be my toes that bore the scars.

The ability of a horse to manoeuvre a cart is impressive. We were able to back into corners and round bends that no tractor and trailer would attempt. But that was the least of the advantages for, above all, when I was on my own with a horse I found I had a friend to talk to. He didn't say much in reply, but I guessed he was thinking a lot. I wondered if such sentiment was perhaps a mistaken approach. I cannot remember Gerry, a horseman of the old school, ever saying a kind word to a horse through any of those long winter muck-carting mornings. It was always, 'Guurrrt on, horse . . . youuu . . . bloody hoss . . . guuurrt on. . . .' Then he'd pause. 'How many loads was that, how many?' he would ask again. It turned out to be no idle question. There was a highly tuned biological time-clock ticking away inside Gerry and he knew precisely how many loads from breakfast to mid-morning cup of tea and from tea to dinner-time. When we hit the magic number he was away across the fields like a startled rabbit, heading for the Rose and his lunch of nut-brown ale.

# Four

IT took me very little time to adapt to the pace of farm work for, as I had already learned, it is dictated by the speed of the horse, which seems to me to be a natural pace at which to work. Economically it might be a disaster on a modern farm of prairie-like proportions; it would take a fair chunk of a harvest season just to walk around a thousand acres with a Suffolk horse. But when Suffolks were kings of the land, farms were the size of Weylands – and I tell you, the scale of it feels right.

There was something about the style of Weylands Farm that was changing me. The sheer burden of repeated bending with the muck-fork meant that I found the stoop, the shuffle and the rounded shoulders of the old farm-hands came ever more naturally. The farmer's boy was ageing rapidly.

In the early days I would sprint up the slippery path to the cattle pen to deliver the early morning feed, clutching a heavy sack or bucket of corn; but within a few weeks I learnt that anything other than a measured pace was a waste of effort. A hasty pace forward meant an equally speedy slither backwards; so I learned to take it slowly and get there just as quickly, the philosophy of a true landsman. In those dormant days of winter, I cannot remember feeling any sense of urgency except when the morning tea-break was approaching. Then we would not

31

want to be far from the house in case we failed to hear the call.

Having made all these personal adjustments of pace, both in mind and body, I easily became resentful about intrusions into the timelessness of the place. I found that the approaching rattle of a diesel engine, heralding more horses for shoeing, became an irritation. They hissed their brakes and revved their engines as they manoeuvred in the yard. Some were as big as long-distance coaches, and when they had finally switched off the engines the blaring stereos continued to obliterate the silence. I would give the drivers a scornful look, as you might at a man who was playing a transistor radio in church.

I wonder what the horses thought of it all. Prince would stand, motionless and obedient as ever between the shafts of his tumbril, having been told to 'stand still, hoss', while out of these luxuriously appointed mobile horse-homes would gaily trip ballerina-like thoroughbreds and spirited showjumpers; flighty gymnasts descending amongst heavyweight boxers. Some would rear and plunge as they came down the ramp, others would need two men pulling on each side to get them back up it again. And Prince would still be standing, not moving an inch. All he would need would be a 'guurtt on, hoss' and he would ease his mighty shoulders into the collar, the leather would creak, the chains scrape as they went taut, and the muck-cart would make its way back up the hill again. From the horsebox came the sounds of nervous dancing as these unsure visitors pranced impatiently on the spot. 'A dreadful waste of energy,' Prince must have been thinking to himself.

Apart from being an agricultural backwater, Weylands Farm was also a cultural centre. Those whose hearts

reposed in days gone by came here for spiritual refresh-
ment, or simply to share the likeminded company –
amongst them a wart-charmer.

There is much superstition surrounding the working of
the land and the care of horses. I had had flashes of it in
conversational throwaways by Roger: 'He makes up this
mixture, and do you know, that horse only had to smell it
and he'd be right as rain. . . .' 'Old Charlie over at so and
so, he had this medicine he made up. Ah! that was good
that was – best thing for a horse, but he'd never say what
was in it. . . .' None of this is to be found in veterinary
manuals, and it has hardly ever been recorded in print.
But much of it is still safe in the minds of the eternal
characters who regularly pass through the kitchen at
Weylands Farm. Sit there long enough yourself, and a
compendium of country wisdom and culture will reveal
itself before you.

It was the visit from the hairdresser that had at-
tracted the wart-charmer. It would be foolish to think that
Cheryl or Roger would waste valuable time sitting in a
hairdresser's shop when there was work to be done on
the farm, so the hairdresser came to them and did their
hair and anybody else's who happened to be around.
Ladies were running around with towels round their wet
hair like startled hens after a shower of rain, and Roger
was having his flat cap with the broken peak prised from
his head and a few snips taken before he had the chance
to escape back to his forge.

Claude, the old wart-charmer, sat in silence while his
thin silver hair was trimmed. In fact, I cannot remember
him saying one word all the time he was there. I don't
even think he bothered with a goodbye – unusual for him,
so they said. Only later, over the dinner table, was the

breadth of this man's talents revealed. Roger told the story with great relish, for Roger with a good tale is a sight to behold. You can spot a good one coming a mile off. He will lean back in his chair, then a smile prompted by a recollection in his mind will cross his face and he will stare out of the window as he tells it.

'I was down at Claude's the other day. He dresses pheasants, you know. Well, I went into his front room and there was a dozen of 'em, all lying round the edge of his dining table with their heads hanging over the side. There was blood dripping from 'em. He'd put little tin trays underneath to catch the blood, he 'ad. That's true, that is!' and he chortled in disbelief at his own story. I waited.

'Well, he was sitting there in his old armchair with a pheasant on his knee, feathers flying everywhere and his sleeves rolled up and 'e'd got rags round his wrists soaked in paraffin. I said, "What yer got them rags for, Claude?" He says, "To keep them bloody lice from running up m' arms and going over m' head like a gang of harrows." He bloody well had, too. Them old birds, they were lousy as cuckoos, lousy as cuckoos they were.' Roger laughed ever louder. 'I said, "Why you plucking them buggers, them's as rotten as hell?" He said, " 'Cos her at house wants 'em plucked, that's why!" ' We laughed. 'But that old devil, he can charm warts, you know.'

I looked at Roger, and there must have been a hint of scepticism flash across my face. He leaned back in his chair. We were in for another cracking tale.

'We had a horse here. That had a big wart on its neck size of a saucer, that must 'av bin. Size of a saucer! Great big thing it was. Well, that horse, that had been to Newmarket to have tests and God knows how many vets had taken bits here and there but that wart, that just

34

wouldn't budge. Well, old Claude, he was here having his hair cut and this horse came in for shoeing. I said, "You jus' go an' 'ave a look at that there wart." Well, he went out, looked at it for a bit and said, "I carn't promus nuthin, but I'll do mar best." '

'Did he touch it?' I asked.

'No,' said Roger. 'He just looked at it, and do you know . . .' everyone in the kitchen, even though they must have heard this tale a dozen times before, went silent with attention '. . . that wart was *gone* in three weeks.' We all shook our heads.

'Now, we don't know how he does it, but I've heard that these old boys go home and they bury a lump of meat and do something to it, I don't know what. But you mustn't ask, 'cos if they tell you how they does it, then their power passes to you.'

I looked forward to Claude's next haircut. Perhaps he might bring a flagon of the potent wine he is alleged to brew. He is known to have turned up at Weylands and offered it round at seven-thirty in the morning, and after only a modest draught Roger has found himself unable to shoe a horse that day.

'Christ knows what it was,' said Roger, leaning back again in his chair. 'Mangel-wurzel wine, I reckon.'

Laughter over the dinner table once again; laughter in the warm, an abiding memory of winter meal-breaks when every story delayed the moment of returning to the damp frosty air and the chilling touch of the steel shaft of the muck-fork.

# Five

FEBRUARY was a tantalising month. The ground would freeze hard for days on end, and then the wind would swing from the chilling east into the milder and damper west. As soon as the thaw spread through the soil, the land would cry out for work to be done. Then the ice and snow would return and portents of an early spring would vanish once again.

By the end of January there were still fifteen or more acres to plough in parts of the farm I had not yet even seen. Ploughing is a fundamental act, and dangerously and misleadingly picturesque. The thought of it can bring a sentimental glow to the townie's heart, but real-life execution of it brings something more like tears of pain to those, like me, who are new to the ways of this basic and elemental piece of farm equipment: the plough.

Ploughs lay scattered around Weylands Farm. There must have been half a dozen of them, mostly blue and recently painted, but some just rusty. They would be at the end of an abandoned furrow high on a hillside as if, for some calamitous reason, the ploughman had had to flee the field with his horses. The real reason is much less sinister: ploughs are simply left where the day's work ends, and from that point the following day's work will start, if the weather allows.

Rupert and Thomas were in plough harness. Thomas

was Roger's best and favourite ploughing horse. He usually ploughed alongside Toby, but it was old Rupert's turn today. Plough harness has no saddle to put across the horse's back, since ploughing is pulling rather than carrying work: all that is needed is the stout padded leather collar and a pair of long chains which will eventually hook the two horses to the plough. A light strap goes across the horse's back simply to stop the chains scraping along the ground. Cart-horses seem so much easier to deal with than spirited light horses, and so much less unpredictable in their ways, that one is forced to the conclusion that they are more intelligent. It would be a brave man who would lead a pair of light horses alone on the end of one lead, but with Suffolks this did not feel at all a risky business.

Roger clipped a light chain from Rupert's bit to a ring at the back of Thomas's harness. This simple but highly effective device means that the horses will walk together as an easily controllable pair. If Thomas slows down, the pull on Rupert's bit will slow him too. If, on the other hand, Rupert wants to get a move on, he can speed Thomas up by a good tug. All Roger had to do was walk in front, showing the way and occasionally urging them on up the steepish hill that led to the highest of the fields at Weylands – Wheeping Hills.

'I wouldn't give that hoss to a boy,' said Roger, pointing towards Thomas as we walked. 'He can be difficult, he can.'

There seemed to be two classes of worker on a farm: horsemen and boys. Boys might be in charge of a pliable horse, the sort you would put between the shafts of a muck-cart. Horsemen were needed to exert their authority over horses like Thomas. Indeed, horsemen were the crown princes on farms in the days when horses ruled. The 'guv'nor' was the farmer or landowner, for whom they all worked, but the head horseman was not far behind in the pecking order, even though he was an employee, and he had distinct rights of precedence over all other horse-men. It would be his sole privilege to be first to leave the stable yard when more than one team of horses went out to plough. Equally, it would be his word that would be law when it came to working the horses on the fields.

'Look!' cried Roger, pointing to the sky with the hand that wasn't leading Rupert and Thomas. 'That old gull, he knows when we're a going ploughin'.' Sure enough, a lone seagull was circling overhead, and had been since shortly after we had left the stables. His keen eye had spotted the horses. It was clever of him to recognise the harness as being plough harness rather than trace or cart harness; it was more than I could have done at that early stage in my agricultural education. He circled over us as we moved towards Wheeping Hills, and before long he was joined by a friend, and then a flock, until several score were squawking for action by the time we got to the top of the hill.

'The best way to learn to plough is on a snowy day,' said Roger. 'You don't need any horses. Just set up a stick at the other end of a field and walk towards it in as straight a line as you can. When you get to the stick, look back and see how straight your path was. You can't plough straight if you can't walk straight.'

The view from the top of Wheeping Hills was amongst the finest I have seen in inland Suffolk. The river valleys of the Box and the Stour carved through the hills to the south and west; to the north were the wooded hillsides of the estate of which Weylands Farm was part. The weather had been mild, so the sandy soil was easy on the feet; but during that morning the wind had swung to the north and freshened, so that by mid-afternoon it penetrated as many layers of clothing as it had a mind to.

Half of this rolling field had already been ploughed, not simply by starting at one end and working towards the other as you might expect, but in strips, or 'stetches' as Roger called them. These strips were then joined up until they became one completely ploughed field. I could not quite see how or why, but even an untrained eye could spot from the different shades of chocolate-coloured earth where one day's ploughing had finished and the next had begun. The ploughed parts of the fields were as regular as newly woven corduroy.

The aged plough was made by Ransomes, a famous Suffolk manufacturer of farm machinery. Their name was stamped proudly down the two handles. There were two wheels at the front, one larger and one quite small: one to run in the furrow, the other to run higher on the unploughed land. Moving backwards along the length of the plough, next came a short spade like affair called a 'skimmer'. This runs along the surface of the unploughed land, scraping off a thin layer of stubble or weed and throwing it to one side so that it is covered with soil and buried out of existence when the plough pours a slice of earth over it. Then came the 'coulter'. This is a vertical knife which cuts the upright side of the slice of earth that the plough is to turn over. Then, a couple of inches behind, the leading edge of the mould-board, the wave-shaped piece of cast iron which actually turns the earth. The tip of this is the hard iron 'plough-share' itself, and this cuts horizontally before curving upwards, so that, together with the coulter, a block of earth is first cut before the mould-board comes slithering along to turn it over.

'Stand there, hoss,' ordered Roger. Not shouted or barked but merely stated, and the horses obeyed and stood by the head of the plough and gazed into the far distance, or as much of it as their blinkers allowed them to see. Roger strode off to the far end of the field and the horses watched. Until he gave another command, they would not move; in the minutes that he was away, not one muscle flinched except for the heaving of their mighty chests, still puffing after the long climb up the hill.

Roger returned with a stick with a white rag tied round the top of it. Then he paced and counted to himself as he walked, stopped when he reached some magic number and then decisively rammed the stick into the ground. Then he strode back to the far end of the field and once again counted the same number of paces from the last furrow that had been ploughed, and rammed another stick into the earth. Then he came back to where the horses and I were standing, rapt. More gulls were gathering in anticipation.

The drawing of the first furrow on a new piece of land has always been a sacramental task. It was never delegated nor undertaken lightly, for a head horseman's reputation would depend on it. A man who could not plough a straight furrow was a man who counted for nothing. You were as good as your furrow, and if it was less than perfect it was an enduring shame: nothing could conceal the meandering of the plough and it would be there for all to see till young green growth concealed it – one season of shame.

So, with the reputation of generations of ploughmen

weighing heavily on his shoulders, and with concentration that would do justice to Euclid scribing a line, Roger set his horses along the line of the two sticks. He spoke quietly, like a man whose mind was totally occupied.

'In them old ploughing matches, you know, those boys, they used to go out there and draw a furrow, and they reckon that if that deviated more than seven-tenths of an inch in its whole length, that weren't no good.'

There is a length of rope that goes from the bits in the horses' mouths back to the plough within easy reach of the ploughman's hands. It is called the plough line and acts as a pair of reins for driving and guiding the horses. Rupert and Thomas, however, needed no such physical direction. Words were enough.

'G'up,' called Roger and, as if by some faultless remote control, the two horses took up the drag of the plough on their huge collars and set off down the imaginary line between the two sticks that was about to become the first furrow.

'Walk behind me,' called Roger. 'If you walk alongside you'll catch my eye and distract me.' As soon as the plough had bitten the earth the furrow started to take shape. I stepped into it as fast as any gull and, like any jolly fellow, I followed the plough.

This was sandy land, not the hard, unyielding clay for which parts of Suffolk are famous, and so the plough bit easily. As it scythed through the ground, the soil swished with the crash of a wave and turned a perfect slice of earth. Like the wake of a ship, or the vapour trail of a high-flying plane, it had to be watched in case, during a glance away, it might change its perfect form. Stones were cast aside as easily as earth, and the swooshing noise was occasionally broken by a sharp ring as a stone hit the

41

plough-share. And the horses marched on, unguided by voice or hand.

Following in the furrow was not as easy a stroll as I expected. It is not quite wide enough to walk with each foot side by side, and so one foot is in the depths of the furrow while the other is on the heights of the un-ploughed land. It means that you have to watch where you're treading, and I found this frustrating when all I wanted to watch was the plough and the horses. The horses themselves seemed to manage their feet quite easily, though.

'Cup, cup,' muttered Roger, the order to his horses to move to the left: no more than that, no pull on the rope.

'Woooahh,' he called softly as we reached the far stick, and the horses stopped in unison. Roger looked back and gave his furrow a long hard stare. It was white now down all its length with screaming, ravenous gulls. I had been concentrating so hard that I had not heard them descend, even though they must have flocked on to the ground the instant the plough had turned it over.

The furrow was as straight as my eye could detect. 'That's not too bad,' was as far as Roger would allow himself to go, and then for the first time he took hold of the rope and gave the horses a guiding tug. 'Wheesh . . . wheesh . . .' he urged them, and they side-stepped to the right until they were pointing in the opposite direction, but still standing on the same spot. As they turned, Roger chose his moment and put his weight on the handles so that the plough lifted from the soil; he guided it round so that most of its huge weight was carried round by its own momentum. Get the timing wrong and you would have the whole mass of the iron plough on your hands and 180 degrees through which to turn.

Roger talked of 'splitting' and 'shutting up' and described circles in the air as he tried to explain how the first furrow was then ploughed again, and then again down either side till it became a 'top' and then the ploughman would go in circles round that till it had been 'shut up' to the adjacent stetch. I was lost, so I watched and listened and hoped that I would eventually understand.

It became clearer when I saw it happen. Roger put the tip of the plough on the spot where it had cut the first furrow, but now, of course, pointing in the opposite direction since we were at the opposite end from which we had started. 'G'up,' Roger called, and off we marched, Roger's hands lightly on the plough's handles, just guiding, hardly steering or pushing. The soil swished and the stones sang out some more. Because the plough always throws the soil to the right, we had effectively cut a trench by going down the line we had already drawn.

Then Roger stopped, halfway along the line, and looked back. He compared what he was ploughing with the previous furrow, and took up the rusty spanner which was resting in a socket on the handles of the plough. He gave a nut a turn or two and raised the furrow wheel by a fraction.

'You shouldn't have to fight the plough at all. That plough, that should go on its own if you let go of the handles.'

'G'up,' and we marched on. Then we stopped. Roger made comparisons with the previous furrows and took the spanner to the plough with as much delicacy as a mechanic tuning up a six-cylinder engine. There was never any suggestion of a 'that would do' approach. Either a furrow had been drawn properly or it hadn't, and if the second was not parallel to the first there would be no use shrugging it off, for it was sure to catch up with you. When one stetch met the next, that was the moment of truth. It is not like the wallpapering of a room; if the first piece isn't upright, the last piece isn't going to be.

'Them furrows have got to be level too or that seed won't all be buried at the same depth and you'll get some bits ripening before others, and we don't want that. Do you want a go?'

I was offered the plough and we slithered on our way. The plough bit into the earth and I watched the furrow-wheel with such intent that I did not have a chance to work out where my feet were falling. Walking in the furrow thus ceased to be a problem; my feet did the thinking for me. 'Just press on the handles and steer it, don't fight it, just guide it. Cup, cup . . . Thomas. Gurt on, hoss!'

I cannot say how long the furrow was. It took only five or six minutes to walk the whole distance, but both horses and this particular ploughman needed a rest at the end of it. It was probably tension on my part, stress through not wanting the plough to waver an inch and therefore steering more than was necessary, added to an instinctive desire to be pushing the plough, which is a total waste of effort. But I was pleased with my first furrow. It felt straight and sure and only at the end had I made a major break from the straight and narrow. But what's a foot in a field as big as this? Then I looked behind me. In fact, it was as wavy as if drawn by a drunken horse and driver, compared with Roger's ruler-straight furrow next to it. Even the gulls didn't seem as keen on this furrow as on some of the others.

'That's not too bad,' said Roger, 'but that's a hard job to get your work just right,' and he kicked loose earth over the foot of land where my plough had jumped out of the furrow. He couldn't bear the sight of even a tiny mistake in his beautifully ploughed field.

Then I ploughed some more while Roger guided the horse, and after a couple of 'rounds' or circuits of the stetch I was able to relax and enjoy the crash of the earth as it fell away from the plough and the beautiful precision with which the horses' feet fell exactly into the furrow: a mark of a true and well-bred Suffolk horse. We all sweated together after a few more rounds.

'That must be gettin' near four o'clock,' said Roger. 'That old hoss, he's gettin' awkward. He don't like to plough much after four o'clock. That's his regular feed-time.' And as he spoke, Cheryl appeared over the brow of the hill clutching Thermos flasks of tea. She looked cold, almost frost-bitten.

'I've been sitting in that meadow with an old ewe who didn't look too well. I thought she might be havin' a bit of bother with her lamb but she's gettin' on all right,' and she rubbed her hands to warm them. We all felt the chill now. The wind was settled in the north and the sky was filling with grey cloud that looked laden with snow. The sun was gone. Rupert and Thomas munched a handful of grass that Roger had picked for them and we supped our tea and gazed out over the modest patch of land that we had ploughed. Despite its lack of precision or military line, I was proud to have done it. As Roger called 'G'up' to the horses and headed them for home, for the first time it crossed my mind that to be atop a Suffolk hill, behind a horse-drawn plough, was as near to total peace as a man might wish to be.

# Six

FOR all the days of glorious discovery there were days of toil and drudgery. Even to a newcomer, fired with enthusiasm and fulfilling a dream of working on a farm, the endless round of fetching and carting palled. Perhaps it is only the prospect of the changing seasons that has kept men on the land: the sure knowledge that whatever today may be like, in only a few weeks' time they are certain to be sweating under a harvest sun; or that however much they may bake in the current heat, there will surely be fresh days following the plough in a month or so.

When I arrived at seven, water-carting was my first job. All buckets and troughs were filled so that when the horses returned to their stables after work, there would be gallons for them to drink. And gallons they needed too. It is hardly possible to believe the amount that a Suffolk takes in one gulp. Even the level in a deep and wide trough falls visibly with every draught.

That job done, I would water the sheep who were in a lambing pen at the back of the yard. Roger had built a thatched roof over part of it, for he liked to lamb as early as Christmas so that his best pure-bred Suffolk lambs could be plump enough by the summer to win prizes at the county shows. The thatch kept mother and lamb warm. They needed watering too. Some mornings all that was necessary was for the ice to be broken on the troughs, but when the cold bit deep and the pipework froze, water had to be carted from the house.

Other mornings, Gerry would be grinding away at some huge, cast-iron mincer of a machine; big enough to mince a man if he happened to fall in it. He was flinging (or as near to flinging speed that he ever got) huge, ruddy, swollen vegetables the colour of grossly mutated radishes, weighing about six pounds each.

'Them's mangels,' said Roger, appearing suddenly from the forge. 'They say that they're eighty per cent water, but that's bloody good water! The horses love it.' He chortled and was off to see his pigs. Gerry ground on, a binful of sliced sweet-tasting mangel gradually filling at his feet. 'Unchokable' boasted the machine on its aged iron work. Gerry coughed heartily as he wound the handle.

We shovelled some more muck out of the yard that morning. It was again Prince's turn in the tumbril, as it seemed to be every time we had muck to shift. We piled it high, about a ton of it, and instead of heading for the muck-heap, we took it down to the garden of one of the big houses in the village; some favour was being repaid with a load of nutritious horse-muck for the rose beds. Gerry was leading Prince, and fumbled to light a damp stub of cigarette as well as lead the horse in a straight line. Consequently we cut the corner a bit fine as we turned into the distinguished entrance gates and the stately stone balls atop the brick gateposts rocked ominously as we scraped by. The same sort of balls had been placed at intervals along the edge of the gravel drive to deter wandering cars, but Prince just kicked them aside as Gerry let the tumbril meander on to the manicured sward.

When the weather is against you it doesn't take many

more upsets to bring everything to a standstill. Roger had twisted his knee and this set the tone of the day. 'I'm having the vet look at this blasted knee tomorrow,' he insisted, and chose his steps carefully as he made his way across the icy yard. Gerry seemed in a worse mood than usual and had no good word for any horse, so I stayed well out of his way and carried on my rounds with the grooming brush. Temper is infectious, and the mood had spread to the horses, who twitched and tossed their heads as I brushed them.

There was a young Shire horse who had just arrived for breaking and was settling into his new quarters and getting used to bending to the will of Cheryl rather than pleasing himself. He rolled his eye when anyone passed, and in a fit of pique tossed his head and snapped his leather halter clean off. That had to be replaced.

Then a lorry-load of young ponies arrived to be shod, and played and fought like a busful of silly schoolgirls. It ended in tears, as these things always do, with violent kicking matches which the young Shire horse tried to join in. To keep an edge on the atmosphere, Roger was in the forge with a huge rasp and was grinding away at a horse's back teeth with a squeal that had nerves jangling for miles around.

Cheryl was missing that morning. Flu had brought her down. It must have been a powerful kind of bug, more powerful than a one-ton Percheron or Shire horse, for nothing of that size had ever floored her. However, it meant no fried breakfast that day and no mid-morning tea either. Things were really bad.

One of the first things I always asked Gerry when I arrived for my weekly day's work was what he had been up to during the week when I wasn't there. He always replied, 'Oh, jus' odd jobs, odd jobs yo' know. Jus' messin' about really, messin' about.' I found it an irritating reply at first but soon began to see the sense in it. Not all farm jobs had the romantic air of ploughing about them. There *were* jobs that were just messing around; simple routine jobs that had to be done, but after which you felt that nothing had been advanced. Straw-fetching for bedding down sheep, carting huge bulbous mangels from the heap at the bottom of the field, muck-shifting, and what Gerry called 'squaring-up'.

Squaring-up is a useful activity. Gerry was a firm believer in it and told me that his father before him had told him that a job wasn't done till you'd squared-up after you. It usually involves much shuffling around with the four-pronged fork, but is basically no more than tidying up after you've finished. If we had been fetching mangels off the storage heap, or 'clamp', we would go back and 'square-up' by putting back the straw thatch that kept the mangels fresh and securing the tilts (tarpaulins) that kept the rain off. Needless to say, if dinner-time was only half an hour away and it didn't seem worth the effort of starting another job, 'juss squaring up' was a handy time-filler, or waster.

I trod carefully on Friday the 13th. A young Clydesdale, a member of yet another noble breed of heavy horse, had arrived; she was there to be broken to harness and her first day at school was not passing without incident.

There is a yard on the farm, about the size of a tennis court, which has high boarding all around and loose boxes at one end with a deep bed of straw across the ground. This is where the horses are turned out at night and where, during the day, Cheryl schools youngsters.

Nan hadn't even got as far as the first lesson. She had been tied up on her own by a stout rope to an old railway sleeper that was buried up to half its length into the ground. The young and fit Nan had no trouble removing that with one jerk of her unruly head and was proudly parading around the yard with several hundredweight of tarred wood dangling on the end of her tethering rope. Gerry cursed. He knew it would be his job to put the post back. Cheryl cursed, realising that this horse didn't have even basic manners, for when they tried to tie her up again she gave a repeat performance. Being tethered is the first lesson a young horse has to learn.

Roger was called for. He took a length of rope and approached the horse with some stealth. With carefully considered movements and many reassuring words to the horse – 'Good lass . . . good lass . . . good girl' – he slipped a rope round her belly and tied it with a slip knot. The loose end he then gently brought up to the rope halter and knotted the two. The young horse stood trembling as if about to explode.

'Before the year's out,' whispered Cheryl, 'you'll see a horse like this go berserk. If that happens, there's only one thing to do and that's clear off out of it as fast as you can.'

Roger took the loop of line that joined the halter and the rope girth and carefully slipped it over another upright railway sleeper – this one set in concrete. He dived out of the way as the horse pulled back and found that nothing gave. Quite the reverse – the more she pulled, the more the girth tightened, but her young mind was unable to grasp the relationship between cause and effect.

'Sometimes they buck and kick and go wild,' said

50

Cheryl, 'but this one ain't too bad. Now watch.'

Roger crept up to the horse as she stamped her feet and threw her head around. He waited till she settled a little and then screamed and roared, waving his hands, shaking his coat. I can't speak for the horse, but I was certainly no brave Daniel in this lion's den and I looked around for some cover. Then Roger took off his flat cap and advanced upon the horse, waving the cap until he was close enough to box the horse's ears. The horse grew wilder and more cross. Roger shouted some more. Then he picked up an old bit of sacking and repeated the performance, until a magic point was arrived at where the horse's temper started to cool. She threw herself about less and less. Roger gave one last enormous outburst of shouting and jeering, but there was no violent reaction this time. She stopped pulling on the rope, and stood and watched. He threw the sack over her head but she didn't seem bothered.

'She'll do,' Roger declared, and went off to breakfast. The young horse was carefully tied up and behaved herself perfectly for the rest of the day.

To mark the end of the winter's work and what we dearly hoped would be the beginning of the spring season, we sowed some beans. Not broad beans for the table, but feed beans to be harvested, crushed and fed to cattle.

It is a bridge between the two farming seasons – the end of the long, hard ploughing and the optimistic sowing of the new seed – for the beans are sown simply by the passing of the plough. As the furrow is cut, the bean seeds are dropped into it from a wooden hopper that dangles between the two handles of the plough. As the adjacent furrow is cut, the slice of earth topples over the seed: ploughing and sowing in one efficient operation.

The field was down in the valley, the river forming one of its borders. It was a good fifteen acres and had not been ploughed before by Roger and Cheryl, so gaps had to be cut in hedges to allow teams of horses through, and ditches had to be filled with rubble to get the ploughs across. A man I had not seen before was surveying the field with a keen eye. He was Jim Young, a revered old ploughman and farmer whose heart still lies in a well turned furrow.

'There ain't many people I respect at doing this job,' Roger once told me. Jim Young is one of them. This stooping but fit figure of a man had a habit of suddenly appearing and taking over at the plough. Cheryl might be happily ploughing away when Jim Young would arrive. He would stride across the field and, to save him asking, she would always offer him the plough. He would take hold, call to the horses and bend himself over his plough as he made his way down the field. Then he would turn, and look, and plough on. Cheryl would be left standing while he renewed his love affair with the furrow.

'If he don't like the way a bit's been turned over,' Cheryl told me, 'he'll go and pat it smooth with his hand.' He ploughed with the precision of a man smoothly icing a cake: no blemish was going to mar his day's work. And if someone else's furrow was not as straight as he would like, he would go and sort it out for them, as he did for Cheryl on a couple of occasions. Not many would get away with that, but Jim Young can. He keeps his own plough at Weylands Farm. 'That's Mr Young's plough,' they say as you pass by and pay it due respect.

The importance of the straightness of the furrow

52

crossed my mind many times. I felt certain in my own mind that the only harm a wavy bit of ploughing could do was to the pride of the man who did it, and not to the crops the land was intended to grow. I asked Roger, and he spoke of 'drainage' or 'gettin' it right when you're drillin' '. But I noticed an added keenness in the ploughing when the ploughed field would be clearly visible from the road, so I came to the conclusion that craftsmanship, pride and good husbandry were close relations in this matter.

I strode with Jim Young down to the field by the river which had been meadowland until quite recently. Roger had drawn out the furrows which determined where the stetches would be, but this was clearly some time ago, as they were well overgrown with weeds. Jim Young started to pace out the field, still able to talk while counting in his head.

'How do you become a good ploughman?' I asked.

'You just get on and do it, and always have good hosses. There ain't nothing to it really.' He started to mutter under his breath, 'That's three hundred yards. . . .' He took some more giant strides, muttering numbers under his breath as he walked. 'That's so many rods to the acre . . . a hundredweight of beans will do . . . that's two thousand times . . .' and this interminable calculation went on until he arrived at a magic figure. He paused for breath, chewed his top lip for a moment and then announced, 'That will need four and a half pounds of beans to every row!' And he marched back to the farmhouse with his news.

The day that we eventually started to plough in earnest did not get off on the best footing, for me anyway. The last of the lambs was born that morning, which in itself was a sign that spring might be around the corner. But a seasonal spirit had not filtered through to the flock of aggressive, grumpy geese that Cheryl asked me to feed. Even as I approached, the cursed things tautened their long white necks and hissed loudly. Then they advanced towards the wire netting, bent on some kind of attack and seeing me not as the bringer of sustenance but as an invader of their territory. As far as I was concerned, they were welcome to their stinking muddy little patch of earth beneath a few bare trees at the back of the barn. I had no designs on it whatsoever, but one gander had designs on me. He flapped till he was airborne and over the low fence, and took hold of my arm in his beak. It hurt. He hammered away till I repelled him with a huge belt round the head with the metal bucket. I threw the food at the rest of them, cursed them in foul language and turned to see a chortling Roger and Cheryl. 'We sent a young boy in there the other week, and those geese, they had him up the tree.' And they laughed some more.

This left my attacker free and wandering around the outside of the pen, unable to get at the food I had thrown in there. I would quite happily have left the bird to starve to death, but Roger took up a pitchfork and advanced with confidence upon the goose. He snared it by trapping its neck between the two prongs of the fork which he then pressed through the netting. It didn't hurt the goose in any way, but it was surely trapped.

'Once you've got their necks, then you've got 'em,' Roger told me, and with his hand now gripping the goose's throat, he was able to lift the bird up and dump it over the fence. It hissed some more, but not as much as I hissed back at it.

After breakfast, the horses were 'collared-up'. Roger

shod a horse while Gerry hunted for harness like an old lady at a jumble sale. Gerry and I were to have a pair of young horses, Nelson and Gedge, which Cheryl had just broken to harness. Roger was to plough with three abreast and Cheryl with a pair. We stood and waited till Roger had finished in the forge, for it was his traditional right to be first on to the field. 'That'll be raining soon,' Gerry said, and we set off as soon as Roger had led his horses away.

I led Gedge, a young horse and not as easy to lead as some of the older and wiser animals like Rupert. He bucked a little and had to be held back, but the older horses knew that there was a hard day's work ahead and didn't rush to meet it. Gerry had hung his woollen overcoat on the wooden hames that stick up above the horse's collar as a gesture of faith in his weather forecast, and Cheryl asked me to take my box of sandwiches down to the field as it was likely we would be there till the job was done.

The sacks of bean seeds were already on the edges of the field to greet us. I looked at the vast expanse of field; the river meandered around the edge of it and, far from being neatly square, it tapered like a wedge. Even so, it looked as though it would take an eternity to slice it into nine-inch furrows. Gedge and Nelson, our two young horses, did not stand still as well as the others and so we struggled to get them hitched to our plough. Gerry cursed and shouted, Cheryl strolled over and just muttered a word, and meekly they obeyed. 'You want to know anything, you just ask me,' and she went back to her own pair, who were harnessed and anxious to start. Roger hitched his horses three abreast: Thomas and Toby, with Richard in the middle. He was using a plough with two shares side by side and so cut two furrows at once, hence the extra horse-power up-front.

We called, 'Gee up', but my horses stood still. We lashed them with the plough line, but they didn't move; so I went round the front and took hold of the bits in their mouths and led them. One started off before the other and, sensing the other wasn't with him, stopped. By this time, the stationary one had got the message and taken a step forward, but as the other had stopped by now he stopped again too. Then the other tried, and we went backwards and forwards on the spot till I gave them a good pull, and they moved off. But not for long. As soon as I stopped pulling, they stopped walking. And still the unploughed field was staring at us; it was as depressing as facing a hundred miles of motorway with a misfiring car engine.

'That old hoss, he'll go better when he's . . .' and Gerry's voice dribbled into another of his mumbles. I asked him what he had said. He caught the impatience in my voice.

'That hoss will go better when it's had a PISS,' he shouted for the whole field to hear. I may have blushed.

Cheryl sorted us out – 'You don't need no shouting' – and she took up the plough line (never called reins), softly said, 'Come on, boys,' and they pulled away together, sure and steady. The young horses puffed as they pulled the plough through the sticky earth, but not as much as Gerry croaked and wheezed as he fought to keep the plough in a straight line, despite the wanderings of the horses. At the end of each furrow, as we reached the headland, it was my job to turn the horses while Gerry man-handled the plough round. More often than not we would miss, and Gerry and I would end up shouting contradictory orders at the poor horses, adding to the confusion. Meanwhile, Roger and Cheryl went about their ploughing in an orderly and serene way. Then a miracle happened. Gedge came to a halt. Nelson was brought up short by the suddenness with which it happened. Gedge spread his rear legs and, with a cascade of awesome proportions, he relieved himself, as much to the delight of Gerry as to himself. Sure enough, he went better after that.

You might think that a field is just a field, and one furrow no different from the next, but that is not so. Each time the plough bit into the earth it was into a different kind of soil, and before it reached the far end it might have cut its way through half a dozen different earths – some heavy clay lumps, some almost sandy.

'There's no cut in that bit there,' Roger would call as we passed by going in the opposite direction. He was right too. It did not cut well, and instead of leaving a sharply turned furrow it merely crumbled away as the plough slid through it. We stopped occasionally when a stone stuck between coulter and ploughshare, and, more importantly, we stopped when Gerry needed a cigarette. He would dive into the innermost depths of his jacket, pull out some soiled scraps of paper, and light one. I can't even be certain that there was any tobacco wrapped in them; the flavouring the baccy had bestowed on the paper when it had been an entire cigarette was clearly sufficient stimulant for him. He coughed a little, and wheezed even more as he followed the plough up the next furrow.

We rested the horses at every headland, and Roger would take the chance to look around. He spotted a rabbit hole. 'We'll have the old ferret down there,' he warned. Then he smelled a fox. 'I can't describe it, but I just know it. There's been a fox along here. There it is,' and he sniffed deeply. I tried to catch it but caught only the smell of dampness. Gerry was right in his forecast; it started to pour with rain.

This seemed to make Cheryl even cheerier. 'Jim Young always says,' she bellowed from the far end of the field, 'that ploughing is a poor disguise for work.' And she was away into the far damp distance almost singing the commands to her two horses.

It is only when things go wrong that you realise that the horses have minds of their own, otherwise you can come to think of them as remotely controlled machines. I cannot remember exactly what happened, but my eye was following a flock of distinctly rowdy and aggressive gulls. The field had been littered with them ever since we arrived, but this flock seemed noisier and more boisterous than the rest. I followed them with my eye across the field, and saw them come up behind Roger's three-horse team. I heard Roger cry 'whooah' with much more force than usual, but this time the horses did not respond. They started to bolt, breaking into a trot with the plough still trailing behind them. Cheryl stopped her horses and ran to help. Then Richard fell. He dropped like a stone and that brought the other two horses to a standstill. As he tried to get back on his feet, he started to kick out at the others while Roger and Cheryl struggled to free him from the plough. They calmed him with words, and soon he was standing with no apparent damage done.

'He's swoundered,' said Cheryl, 'swoundered hisself.' Gerry looked on.

'Do you say he swoundered?' asked Gerry.

'When the horse in the middle lunges forward and the other two don't go with him,' Cheryl explained, 'the collar squashes his windpipe and he faints. That's why he fell.'

He was fine within a minute, they hooked him back into the plough and five minutes later it was as if nothing had happened.

'Did she say he swoundered?' asked Gerry. I told him she had, and he lit another tobacco-stained slice of paper in celebration of his witnessing a rare phenomenon.

We had our meal break on the headland in the drizzle. Mild rain dripped off our caps into the thick vegetable soup we had brought with us, and we sat on the empty bean-seed sacks and gorged our sandwiches to satisfy a ravenous appetite while the horses just stood, their backs to the wind.

'I used to borrow other people's fields to start with,' Roger told me, 'and I just learnt to plough that way. Then I went to a few ploughing matches and got to know how to do it over the years. I should say the secret's in the plough. I could give you my plough now and you could go out there and make a decent job of it, but that's because I've set it up. If you had to set it up yourself you could get into a muddle. Setting the plough's the secret,' and he wandered off, distracted by another rabbit hole down which he might set a ferret.

The machinery that sows the bean seeds has a biblical simplicity about it. It is funnel-shaped, made out of wood and sits between the handles of the plough. On the bottom is a wheel which runs along the ground, and this turns a smaller grooved wheel which runs through the seed in the funnel-shaped hopper. As it turns, the seed is picked up by the notches in the smaller wheel and dropped on to the ground as it rolls along. Simple and effective.

Roger took a handful of the seed from a sack and held it three feet above the hopper, placing himself so that the breeze was blowing across the top of it. Then he allowed the seed to trickle through his fingers. The heavier seeds fell directly into the machine, while the old seed pods and bits of straw, which would have blocked the machine, were blown away on the wind. Roger smiled. 'Easy way of cleaning seed, that is.'

Onward we trundled, till our feet ached from slithering in the mud. Gedge and Nelson were better behaved, more used to the job now, but Gerry still had a habit of turning the corners sharply and flinging the plough against my leg, so that it felt heavily bruised in several places.

As the stetches grew wider with every passing of the ploughs, the gaps between them narrowed to the point where some serious working-out had to be done. The stetches must meet at the top and at the bottom; they must be parallel, and if they aren't it is as offensive to the eye of a ploughman as a splash of mischosen colour might be to an artist. So when the gaps were down to a couple of yards, Roger paced them out top and bottom and gave orders for any adjustments that might have to be made. We all stood and watched and waited for the verdict. Gerry did some pacing too, but seemed to lose count.

By the time the stetches were shut up, or joined by the last furrow, it was a sight not to miss. We watched as Roger carefully steered the plough to take out any slight lumps or kinks and leave a distinct and straight 'V' of a trench. It was not only a matter of pride; that trench is a highly effective drain which will lead excess rainwater off the field. Its efficiency is as vital to the health of any crop as a dose of fertiliser.

'Takin' up your brew?' bellowed Cheryl down the field.

She turned to me, 'They allus says if you make a good job of takin' up your brew you'll be all right.' The brew, I learnt, is a slight ridge at the bottom of the final furrow which remains when the stetches are shut up. Roger delicately took his plough down it, just skimming it away to leave as perfect a shaped piece of earth as you could wish to see.

With that he called it a day. Exhausted, we all unhooked our horses. Roger tied his in a long line, leapt on the back of the leader and rode up the hill back to the farm. The last job of winter had been done and, optimistically, the first seeds of a new year had been sown. There was little to show for our efforts so far, except for the beautifully manicured earth and a nasty bruise where the damned goose had bitten me.

# Seven

THERE were days when Weylands Farm seemed like the Clapham Junction of the heavy horse world. Horses would be leaving and arriving every other minute: some to start their working lives, others to bring it to a humane close. Those youngsters who arrive for schooling come from all parts of the land; those destined for the knacker's yard join the Clarks' occasional Thursday morning run to the slaughterhouse, laid on for owners who have neither the heart nor the stomach to do it themselves.

The breaking of a heavy horse starts at two years old, when horses wear harness and pull light loads for the first time. Having drummed this routine into their juvenile brains, their masters send them out to pasture for a couple of years to mature, and then they come back for the finer points of schooling. It looks good on paper; in reality it is a highly skilled and dangerous business.

'I more or less learnt it as I went along,' Cheryl once told me as we sat behind a pair of young Shire horses, trotting in orderly fashion along the lane. 'And I sometimes think I'm a fool. I work my guts out to get horses to this sort of standard and then off they go back to their owners, more often than not to be spoilt to death, and I'm left with another mad young sod waiting to be broken in. I don't know why I bother sometimes . . . guurrt on old hoss . . . don't you . . . or I'll. . . .'

The turnover of horses for breaking would make you dizzy. It did me. I would no sooner learn a horse's name and a few of its habits, than it would have been sent home again, fully schooled. Five or six weeks is the time Cheryl takes to break a horse.

'Sometimes, the bad ones just lie down when I try to put the harness on. Just lie down! Well, what use is that? There was one horse who just lay down in the yard, and I could do nothing to get him to stand up. Stupid hoss. So I covered him up with straw. He still had the cart attached to him and I covered that up as well. Still he didn't move. So we left him there. People came and went all afternoon, and no one noticed there was a horse under this heap of straw. About five o'clock he began to stir. I tell you, he was glad to get up, he was. He never lay down in his harness again.' She chortled, and marked up another success. 'There's a trick I've learnt with Shire horses. Cowards they are, most of them. If they lie down I pour cold water in their ears. That gets 'em up soon enough.'

Are there ever any failures?

'I've had horses where I've rung up the owner and said the horse is dangerous and should be shot. I was breaking a Shire for someone and he kept on telling me to persevere with this mad horse. I did what the customer wanted. The horse went home and within weeks he'd been put down. There was no way that horse was ever going to be safe. There's no point trying to break horses that are crazy in the head, no point at all.'

For every aged farm implement that lies around the fringes of the yard, there is a cart that is reserved for the breaking of horses. These are crudely built machines welded out of stout iron rods. They have a plank for a seat and, dangling from a chain bolted to the axle, there is usually an old lorry tyre which gives some drag and makes the horse pull that bit harder. Horses start by learning to pull a sledge – simply a heavy wooden block on two wooden runners. After that, they drag a heavy tractor tyre and then progress to pulling a cart between shafts; finally they learn to work as part of a pair. Only when they have passed that test, both on and off the main roads, will they be considered broken to harness.

'It's a good job some owners can't see what I do. But it's for the horse's good. We had a horse here that nipped and bit you every time you tried to go near it. It had been given endless titbits by its owners, who kept it as a pet. If you didn't give it a sugar lump, it tried to bite your arm off. I soon got it out of that habit [she did not explain how but wore a severe frown] and then, blow me, first thing they do when they come to pick it up is start stuffing it with sugar lumps!'

She shouts at horses with a roar that would freeze any moving thing for miles around; but for every horse that has felt the sharp end of her tongue or even her stick, there is one that has delivered her a few physical blows in return.

'I was out with some stupid horse, and I don't know what happened but it suddenly bolted. Now, a bolting heavy horse is a powerful thing, all right? I was caught off my balance and pulled forward off the driving seat, and when I came to I was across this horse's back. The reins were slack, but I couldn't have stopped him anyway. I thought if I didn't do something soon, I was going to be killed,' she grinned, 'so I pulled what I call my hand-brake.'

The handbrake is a hobble. It is her insurance policy,

which she calls on when all else fails. Two straps are wrapped round the horse's feet near the ankle and connected by a length of line which passes through a small pulley on a strap just below the horse's chest and between its front legs. The other end of the line goes back to Cheryl's hand.

'I just pull it, it's as simple as that. The horse just falls down. It doesn't know what the hell has happened. But if it ever thinks about running away again, it will think twice. When it's been on the ground a bit, we get it up and on we go. They've got pads on their knees. They don't get hurt, but they learn a lot.'

If she wears a stern face when facing up to a stroppy horse, she beams with great delight at her successes. Cheryl will almost break into song on the trudge down the drive after an hour or two with a horse that is willingly accepting its tuition. It is a joy to see the smile on her face when she takes an owner out for a drive with his newly broken horse: it is as if every horse she breaks is her first. And her face crumples in concern when one of her own horses falls ill.

Roger and I were sitting in the yard, on the step up to the barn, scraping the mud and fresh leaf off the sprouting mangels before flinging them into the mangel-grinder. It was a March day, and a not unpleasant job, and we were relaxing in the gentle heat of a welcome burst of sun. Cheryl was just back from a long walk behind a young horse.

'That's clung, that horse is. Clung!'

'Clung?' I asked. They both laughed.

'If you get a lettuce,' said Roger, smiling, 'that's been in its bag too long and it's soggy in the middle, you'd say it was clung.'

'That horse is clung,' Cheryl insisted. 'He's soft and useless. Nothing wrong with him, just a bit soppy, really. Clung.'

'Who do we know who's clung?' asked Roger, still smiling. 'I wouldn't say old, you know who . . . what's his name? But his Dad was a bit clung, weren't he?' and they all roared.

Lynn, the stable-groom, happened to mention that Thomas, one of the Clarks' finest young Suffolk geldings, had been kicking a lot that morning and wasn't touching his midday feed. The laughter instantly stopped. Cheryl ran and pressed her ear to Thomas's side, listening for the gurgling of his gut. If it is silent, there is a blockage, which will be fatal. Roger ran to the house. He returned with a syringe full of an anti-spasmodic drug. Cheryl pressed her ear some more to the horse's belly.

'It might be colic,' she said, looking at a clearly listless Thomas. 'It gives me the jitters, does colic. Old Duke died of colic last year. That was a terrible death. I woke up in the night. I could hear banging and crashing noises. I went to his box. He was flinging himself about. Wild with pain. I couldn't get in there. I rang Philip [the vet] and he was here in no time. He'd stopped off at his surgery to get his gun in case he had to put him down. I couldn't bear to watch the old horse. He was in such pain. He was Supreme Gelding too. Top Suffolk horse. He had a little quiet spell and they managed to get an injection in him, but as he staggered to his feet I looked at his face. I cried, "Oh God, he's going to die. I can't bear to watch," and then he just fell over. Dead. We wouldn't move him, of course. He weighed a ton so we had to get old Rupert harnessed up and Rupert dragged his dead old mate out of the stable. Then we rang for the knacker to come and

66

take the body away, but when he got here there was no way this dead horse was going to go in the lorry. He broke his winch trying to pull him. So they cut him up in the yard.'

'I can always tell when a horse is going to die,' said Roger, 'you can smell it.'

'Smell it?' I asked.

'Yeah, just smell it.'

Then there was silence, almost a minute's silence.

'He's looking better already,' said Roger, whose mind had been on Thomas. 'These drugs, they just relax their old tummies enough to ward off any trouble before it gets too serious.'

'Look,' said Cheryl, delighted, 'he's eating his grub.' And Thomas tucked in, tummy-ache all gone.

After a pause, 'Who else can we think of who's clung?' said Roger, laughing again.

There is as much anguish as pleasure in the keeping of horses, and the Clarks have not escaped without cruel loss. 'We had a horse, Count,' said Cheryl. 'I worshipped the ground that horse walked on. He was a human being, he wasn't a horse. That's all I can say about him. I'm just thankful that once in my life I owned a horse like him. I adored that horse . . .' and her voice tailed off.

One of the finest Suffolk horses of his time, he was struck by lightning while standing in a field.

Those who, like me, pass by Weylands Farm as casual visitors, can never appreciate the heartbreak that is suffered to pay for the apparently simple satisfaction of working the land by horse.

# Eight

SPRING did not arrive with a flourish, it merely gave a suggestion or two that it was not far away. The spring that year was far too mean and tantalising to allow us to enjoy all of it at once. It gave us catkins, but a cold east wind as well; it brought the occasional daffodil into flower, and then snapped it shut again with an icy blast.

The last of the lambs was born. It was a 'gay lamb'.

'They call 'em gay,' said Roger, 'because they've got some odd bits of colouring. A good Suffolk lamb shouldn't have no pinkish colouring like that. There was an old boy round here who was a shepherd. He wouldn't have anything to do with a gay lamb, but he would never say why.'

Chicks were hatched in secret corners of the barn and appeared like rabbits out of a magician's hat. Hens and cockerels run here together in the freest of free-range environments I have ever seen, and who was laying what and where was anybody's guess. Sadly, not all the chicks had much prospect of survival. It was quite usual for the giant foot of Rupert or Prince to fall upon an unsuspecting chick as the horses made their way to the drinking trough, and then to wipe out another one on the way back. So tiny and frail were these chicks that when the huge horse lifted its hoof to take a further step, you would not have guessed that there had ever been a chick there.

The horses sensed that spring was on the way. They fidgeted and rattled at their chains in an impatient way, seeming to sense that life was returning to the meadows and the pastures, and to imagine the flavour of those fresh shoots of grass. With a suggestion of improving weather, we sowed seed as a gesture of our faith that the seasons never failed and spring was sure to arrive.

'Them old boys,' said Roger, 'used to go and sit down on the field they were thinking of sowing, and if they got up and their arses were wet, they'd go home 'cos they'd reckon that old ground weren't dry enough. If they got up and their backsides were dry, they'd reckon they could go ahead and drill.'

The sowing of seed is called drilling, and the machine that puts the seed into the ground is a drill. Roger's was built to be drawn by horses, but even the ones that are pulled by tractor are scarcely different in design. The seed is poured into a large box which runs the full width of the drill, about ten feet. As the drill moves over the ground, the seed is drawn into a toothed wheel, driven by the main wheels. Seed collected in these teeth is then dropped down a series of rubber pipes. It cascades into a small funnel which guides it into a furrow, cut by a revolving disc running just ahead of the pipe. One man drives the horses and the other watches the pipes like a hawk to see that none gets jammed.

We were going to sow oats, or 'utz' as they seemed to be called. Suffolk folk do not seem to take easily to their diphthongs and so the 'oa' in oats is replaced with a 'u' in the same way that the 'ea' in sheaves (as of corn) is replaced by a 'oo'. They talk of 'shooves' of corn.

Be they oats or utz, the sacks were as heavy as I wanted to lift. Tales are told of men who carried so many hundredweight on their backs, but not me. I didn't seem to have the knack. Perhaps it would come with time.

'I like to see the horses' tails tied up when they're working,' said Roger. 'To keep them out of the mud?' I suggested. He paused. 'Just 'cos I think that look right to have 'em tied up.'

So we plaited the tails of Richard, Thomas and Toby, who were to draw the drill. Three horses because, as Roger said, 'I allus prefer to over-horse a job than under-horse it.' We divided the hair into three bundles, starting high up the tail so that our eventual knot of plaited hair would be as high as possible. We then crossed one over the other and the third into the gap between those two, till almost all the hair was used up. Then we gathered two of the three strands together and wrapped them round the back of the tail till they could be knotted at the front. Roger picked up a handful of dry straw and put a few stalks between the hairs as we twisted. 'That won't come undone now,' and he tucked away the loose end. The result: one tight bundle of hair in no danger of getting tangled in the machinery or dragging through the mud.

Roger led Thomas and Toby, while I took Richard. It was cold but sunny, and as soon as we were over the brow of the hill and away from the breeze, it felt warm. Roger took off his overcoat and hung it on the wooden hames on the horse's collar. The ground was dry, and I remember thinking that this was the first time I had set out on this long march to a far field and not slithered at every footstep.

The field we were to drill was a good eight acres in size. It might well have taken well over a week for one man to plough it, but drilling seed is much faster and, although it was now nine o'clock, Roger expected to have this job finished by teatime. We had brought our sandwiches with us in expectation of a full day's work on the land. While Roger hitched the horses, I was sent to fetch the first sack of seed which had earlier been dropped by the edge of the field. I bent, and lifted, and felt muscle fibres stretch and joints click, but with a mighty heave I managed to get the sack up to the height of the seed box, where Roger slashed it with a knife to let the seed pour out. When it was full, we closed the lid and Roger took the lines (reins) in his hand and called 'Gee up' to the horses. There was a sharp squeal as the drill moved off, caused by stones and dried mud rubbing across the discs which broke up the soil for the seed to fall into. But eventually that stopped as the rusty discs started to take on a shine, and we had only gone a few steps when the machine settled down. I could see fine lines of seed left behind us as we trundled on.

The field itself had been ploughed the previous autumn, and had then been harrowed. Harrowing is done by a series of spikes which protrude from an iron framework. As the horses drag the spikes over the ground, the clods and lumps of earth that have been turned over by the plough and have remained unbroken by the winter frosts are crumbled into finer lumps of earth in the same way that a gardener might rake over his patch before planting seed. Harrowing leaves faint lines on the land where the spikes have passed, and Roger explained how you drill at right angles to the lines of the harrow so you can easily see where you've been. Even so, it wasn't that easy.

'That's the first time I've seen a heat haze this year,' he said with some excitement, and pointed to the brow of the hill. Sure enough, the heat was rising and rippling our vision of the trees in the far distance. We stopped and looked as a thirsty man might at a mirage, except that *we*

71

were longing for more heat. But this was still March and we hadn't been staring long at the welcome portent when a chill breeze whistled down the valley and we went back to work to keep warm. Drilling one way was fine; the other way, into the sun, was more difficult. The glare through the slight mist made it difficult to see where we had already passed, and the land was drying so quickly that the browner and damper bits which the drill had turned over soon dried to the grey colour of the rest of the field. But, amazingly, the horses could see where they had been, and with a remarkable display of precision followed the last minute furrow that the drill had cut. To see a horse walk unguided, yet straight and true down a ploughed furrow is remarkable enough, but to see it follow the slightest of lines that a man can hardly discern leaves you with undying admiration for the talents of the working horse.

In a neighbouring field, a farmer was at work with his tractor and harrow. Every crunching change of gear echoed down the valley.

'He's paid twenty thousand for that tractor. Another ten for that power harrow,' said Roger. 'I bought these old harrows at a sale for ten quid and the horses together couldn't have cost more than a thousand. And he won't be home much before we are.' We plodded on, while he chugged away.

'You'll never see corn go in better than this,' declared Roger and, sensing that the elements were on our side, the horses pricked up their ears and eagerly marched forward, dragging the drill till eight acres had been sown.

We arrived back on the farm at about four o'clock to a welcome mug of tea and the arrival, by smoky old lorry, of an advanced piece of machinery. Anywhere else it would have been a museum piece, but on Weylands Farm it was as sophisticated a piece of machinery as you were ever likely to find.

It was a root-chopper, but differed from my old friend the 'Unchokable' mangel-grinder in that it was driven by electricity rather than by Gerry. It also had blades and rollers to strip the mud and sprouting ends off the mangels, thus removing the need for the tomahawk-like knife otherwise used for the job. It was a good thirty years old, if not more, and was six inches bigger than the day it was made, due to a thick crust of bird droppings; but when it was plugged in it gamefully rumbled into life. It was crude, but effective, and as Gerry effortlessly threw in the first mangel, he smiled the smile of a man who has just had a ball and chain cut from his ankle. But the hum of the electric motor, even one that overheated a little and whose pulley system didn't quite fit the drive belt and caused it to slip and emit a distinctive smell of burning, was a new sound at Weylands Farm. The times, and the seasons, they were surely a'changing.

# Nine

SPRING, although not yet heralded by the meteoro-logical portents, was already spreading itself to the corners of Weylands Farm. I arrived one day to find Gerry sniffing the air. He seemed to have more sniffing time on his hands now that he only had to press a button to get his mangels ground, instead of flinging himself at the mechanical grinder. It was a shame in some ways. There was a knack to turning that machine by hand, principally in knowing the moment to let go, otherwise the momentum of the whole thing could carry you round with it. Such ancient wisdom would presumably now be lost for ever.

'That's a good growing day,' Gerry declared, gazing skyward and sniffing some more. I asked why. ' 'Cos that ain't too hot and not too wet, and not so dry either. Just a good growing day.' I was none the wiser but wisdom, although presumably held in great reserves somewhere within Gerry, did not often surface.

'When I was a boy,' he mused, looking at the dwindling heap of uncut mangel, 'we used to go down the pub, drink beer all night and we'd end up drinking half pints of mangel wine.' His face cracked into a broad grin. 'Bloody rough that was. Christ, you felt dreadful the next morn-ing.' Hangovers were milestones in Gerry's life, each to be remembered and recollected with affection.

74

We fed the cattle that morning, and having throughout the winter been in the habit of leaving the gate ajar we did so again. One wilful cow saw her chance and was through; she had to be herded back by a combination of heavy stick and yapping dog.

'They can smell that old grass comin' up,' said Roger. 'Old', I might add, is a word that has nothing to do with age. So we might gather up 'them old lambs' or 'tie up that old fencing' if we felt reasonably disposed to either. The opposite of 'old' is 'bloody', so a cow that had escaped from the field in search of fresh grass was being admired for her cunning if she was 'that old cow, she got out. . . .' But if she had simply been making trouble for all concerned, she was a 'bloody cow that got out'.

I could tell that work had been proceeding well since my last visit by the shine on the normally dull and rusty plough chains. The glint on the inside of the tight links was a sure sign that much heaving and pulling had been done in the previous week, and when I collared Prince and put him to the tumbril I thought I could see a weary look in his eye which suggested that he had spent many hours between those shafts in the last few days. I still approached the whole business of 'collaring' a horse with some nervousness. The size of them held me in some awe. I knew deep down inside that Prince had had his harness on and off his back a couple of thousand times in his life, and never flinched. But what if he took exception this time? What if he felt the collar sliding back over his ears and decided his mid-life crisis was due, and went wild? I would stand no chance, sandwiched between his one-ton bulk and the brick wall. I didn't let the worry spoil the pleasure, but it was always in the back of my mind.

Prince shared a shed with Richard at the back of the yard known as the 'stallion box'. A sore point with them, I would have thought, since both horses were geldings. It was always a muddy walk from this box down past the forge and into the yard where the tumbril lived. It was well watered, not only by the rain that came off the hill behind the farm but also by a free-flowing spring. It was here that the arrogant, vicious flock of geese lived. They hissed and advanced as I made my way to get the horses, but seemed less reluctant to pick a fight when I emerged with either Prince or Richard. Faced with a ton of horse, geese, like me, thought twice about taking chances.

This was not going to be one of those mornings on which some huge chunk of this canvas of a landscape was going to be repainted, either with the broad stroke of the plough or the gentler shading of the seed drill. Rather, it was a day for doing a little touching-up here and there. Gerry busied himself with straw-shifting in the cattle-yard, and with some trepidation I was sent off on my own to cart muck to the big house in the village. This was my first solo trip, the others having been chaperoned by Gerry, and so I felt not only proud at being trusted with a horse and cart and load of muck, but nervous in case the mid-life crisis that had not arrived at collaring-up time might strike Prince halfway down the hill.

Gerry was supposed to help load the cart, but seemed to be otherwise engaged. It was the muck from the sheep pens that we were carrying, and the stench was not as pleasantly aromatic as that of the horse-yard.

'I can't eat lamb, no more,' said Roger. 'When that's cooking that smell just like that muck in that there old yard.' Till he said it, I had not noticed. But he was right and I have never enjoyed a leg of lamb since. I did get pleasure from the muck-shifting, however. I seemed to have missed out on that particular task in the last few weeks, and so it was refreshing to feel muscles yield to the mass of a forkful of sodden, stinking straw. Gerry made a crafty re-appearance just as the last forkful was flung on, and asked if he could help.

I was beginning to learn the words of command which had been imprinted on the minds of all the horses during Cheryl's patient but insistent schooling. The words themselves were quite simple, but the knack was in the delivery. So a gentle 'Gee-up' abbreviated to 'G'up' was enough to get a willing horse on the move; more of a sergeant major's 'GEEEee-uuurrP' might be needed to persuade one of the idler Suffolks to lift his massive feet and take a step forward. Prince was no problem. He even responded to a single word of rebuke, so if he threw his head around in an impatient way, all that was required was a short sharp *'Prince!'* and he would freeze. A good horse, old Prince.

We trundled down the hill on automatic pilot. Roger had told me that a good cart-horse needs no driving, and he was right. He needs leading and showing the right direction, but when it comes to speeding himself up a little to tackle a hill, or holding back when going the other way, a good cart-horse, like Prince, needs no telling.

So relaxing was the half-mile stroll that for the first time whilst in sole charge of a horse I was able to look around and feast on the early days of spring. Trees were thick with buds as bright as jewels and impatient to burst, the very first of the bluebells were just beginning to show between the trees, and flies buzzed round Prince's head – heralds of a long season of irritation for Prince and his stable-mates.

77

Even the 'two old gentlemen' seemed in cheerier mood. These old fellows were the two pure Suffolk rams who lived alone in a field by the house, separated from their wives of the previous autumn and their recent progeny. They stood like restless tribal warriors, knowing that they had a good eight months to wait before they would be reunited with their mates and re-establish their supremacy over the flock. They were proud, hefty examples of the Suffolk breed of sheep, and they knew it. We bade them 'good morning' and trundled on.

I turned sharp left into the gates of the Big House, and took care with my aim so as not to repeat Gerry's gate-post-rattling performance of a couple of months ago. The gardener was ferreting around in the daffodil beds and turned when he heard the first of Prince's feet crunch into his gravel drive.

'I'll tell 'im you're 'ere,' he said and scuttled off to the house. We stood still, awaiting orders. I felt very young, and nervous, like a farm boy being sent out on an errand for the first time, which was not far from the truth. And so when an elderly gentleman appeared on the imposing doorstep, I raised my cap in deference and in salute. It was an automatic reaction.

'Where are you from?' he asked.

I gulped like a young waif, 'Mr Clark's farm, sir.'

'Dump it over there please,' and he pointed beneath a yew tree. We trundled over; the gardener joined us with his fork, and we had unloaded in no time. With no twentieth-century intrusion to destroy this little nineteenth-century scene, I half expected that the gardener might ask me over to the potting shed for a surreptitious pot of tea, or take me into the house for a slice of cook's freshly baked cake. But sadly, no.

The afternoon found us all bent double, as if in prayer. We bent our backs, put our faces towards the earth and walked slowly backwards. We were potato-planting.

'Do you know what variety these are, Tom?' Roger was shouting to a round, grey-bearded fellow who often appeared at Weylands Farm dressed in an orange boiler suit and with a red and white spotted handkerchief tied round his neck. He was one of those men who always had a smile on his face or a ready joke on his tongue. He too kept an old Suffolk Punch that he had saved from the knacker's yard, and she worked on his small farm alongside a collection of rusty nuts and vibrating bolts and smoky exhaust that at one time in its life might have been called a tractor.

'Tom, do you know what variety these are?' Roger asked again as Tom unloaded the sacks of seed potatoes from his trailer.

'Yup, I know what variety they are, all right, guv'n'r,' and with a twinkle in his eye, he sprinted down hill. 'I'm just off to see Cherry for a quick cuppa,' he shouted. 'I'll be back to help you when you've nearly finished.'

He was on a fruitless errand, for no sooner had he disappeared than Cheryl came over the brow of the hill on yet another three-mile training march with yet another student horse, this time a young Shire. She always dressed the same for these daily training hikes: corduroy trousers stitched where the seams had burst, and an old woolly bobble hat pulled down over her ears. If she came into view wearing a smile, then you could assume that the horse had been learning a thing or two and she was satisfied with progress. If she frowned, watch out.

Furrows had already been drawn, and so we simply had the task of dropping potatoes in the bottom, about a foot apart. A foot is a perfect measure for planting spuds. You learn to walk along, drop a potato, and then bring the heel of the foot to where it has fallen, and then aim to drop the next one at the toe. You curse when they bounce and you have to retrieve them and place them in position: it spoils the flow. Centimetres would have been impossible to work out. We carried the seed in big buckets which were sufficient for half a furrow's length, and we then had to walk back to the sacks which were placed at strategic points on the headland. The standing up was harder than the bending double, for it was the straightening of the curved and aching back that really brought tears to the eyes; but when you got used to the bending, shuffling position, it didn't seem to hurt too much.

When two rows had been planted side by side, the horses came along, dragging a special sort of plough which, instead of having one mould-board, had two; so instead of cutting a furrow and throwing the earth to one side, it cut a trench and heaped the earth on both sides. The idea was to drive this implement down the earth between the rows of potatoes, and as it went forward the seed would not only be covered but the displaced earth would form a ridge so that the seed was buried and earthed up in one movement. Master-horseman Jim Young was on one of his regular visits, and so we could expect some ruler-straight furrows and ridges.

'It's a good day for work,' he said, speaking as he often did with a slight whistle in his voice. 'A good day for work' was like the 'good growing day' that Gerry had earlier declared it to be. Jim Young couldn't really tell me what was good about it, but I think I was beginning to understand what he meant. It was not too hot to dry the earth the minute the plough turned it over, neither was it wet enough for the soil to be trampled to clay. There was dampness in the air, but no threat of rain; there was just enough warmth to persuade seeds to sprout, but not enough to bring a working man out in a sweat. I agreed with him. It was a good day for work. Jim Young had come prepared to labour, fully dressed with pigskin leggings wrapped around his ankles to extend the height of his boot and keep mud off his trousers. A landsman's sort of shoe, I thought, and looked down at my miserable, clammy rubber wellies.

'My hosses always go well for him,' whispered Roger as we took a short break from the stooping and the planting, to watch Jim Young take up the lines. He never shouted, never hollered. He just told his horses to 'get on' and they went. His communication seemed to be at a level beyond that which most men could achieve, for when one horse was not lined up exactly as Jim Young wished him to be, he simply said, 'Get in that furrow, go on.' And, as if by magic, the big horse shuffled his feet across till he was exactly where Jim Young wanted him.

'It is my ambition,' shouted Roger, 'to be as good a tradesman as you, Jim.' Jim stopped and looked slightly embarrassed. But to be called a tradesman by Roger was a great compliment, for the work ethic is deeply rooted in Roger. He talked of 'getting your work right' or 'Did you manage to keep your work straight?' when asking about a day's ploughing; and a man who was good at his 'work' Roger called a tradesman, be he horseman, ploughman or farrier. It was the highest compliment in his book.

'Look at that furrow,' Roger whispered, and we moved along a little until we could see along its whole perfectly straight length before it disappeared over the brow of the hill. Its walls were as smooth as if a master

81

plasterer had spent a morning's work with a smoothing trowel. 'You could see a mouse run up that furrow, that's so good, that is.' Roger looked long and hard down that furrow as a young artist might, admiring the work of an old master.

But the old master was quite old, certainly in his seventies, and he rested at the end of each round.

'Farming today,' Jim Young declared, panting a little, 'is a sed-ent-ary occupation,' and he not only spelled out but spat out every syllable. 'They do all the work sitting down in those damned tractors. It would kill some of today's so-called farmers if they had to do this sort of work. None of them would do it, would they?' and he turned to Roger, who shook his head, his attention still taken by that furrow. 'Farmers used to be growers,' Jim went on, taking up the lines ready to start the next round, 'but now they're just converters. They bred their horses to provide the energy they needed and they grew the feed to keep 'em alive. Now they just convert diesel oil and chemicals into crops and that's it. Go on. Get on old hoss. . . .' Crunch went the feet, and the plough swished through the crumbling soil.

'Yup,' said Roger, 'you could see a mouse run up that furrow.'

Not unlike a little furry creature himself, Gerry was scuffling around with another sack of seed potatoes and a bucket.

'You start up that far end and we'll do another couple of rows,' he said. I offered to start at the near end, but Gerry thought the far end was best. So with my bucket I trudged up the hill and bent myself double once again, dropping spuds as I walked backwards. It was a good fifteen minutes before I looked up and discovered the secret of Gerry's masterplan. He was nowhere to be seen. The call of the nut-brown ale had been too strong. Crafty old sod. Never mind, I thought, at least it's a good day for work.

# Ten

THEN Gerry was gone for good. I don't know where he went, or why he went. I didn't ask, and I wasn't told.

Surprisingly, his absence made little difference to the work load, for there were sufficient players in the ever-unfolding rural drama of Weylands Farm to fill any gaps that might unexpectedly occur.

There was Busky, for example, who, according to Roger, 'could do any job on a farm except lay eggs'. Her nickname dates her nicely. 'They call me Busky,' she told me, 'because it was my job to clean the buskins at home.' Buskins are shaped leather leggings worn between the ankle and the knee and not much seen since the 1930s – except on Jim Young. She often wears blue, and packs her greying hair beneath a floppy knitted beret of many colours.

'Blue's a good colour. It doesn't frighten horses, you know,' she told me. This was important, for one of her jobs on the farm is to help Cheryl break horses.

'She's got the patience,' Cheryl said, 'got the patience you need with a young horse. And she loves it, just loves it. It's like a tonic to her.' I often watched her around the yard, just spreading straw or mucking out. It was always the routine jobs that marked out the true farm-workers: the ones who had done it for years and knew what price has to be paid if a task isn't done right. They had the regular jobs down to the finest of arts.

Busky, in her shovelling of straw and muck, always seemed to have a 'good forkful'. Never too much to be unwieldy, or so little that it was hardly worth the bother of lifting the fork in the first place. But her forte, her annual party-piece, was the singling of the mangels. Mangels are usually sown too thickly to allow the plants to grow to full size, so the young seedlings have to be chopped out, leaving single plants a foot apart. It is done with a hoe, and it is one of the few jobs at Weylands Farm that I felt lucky to have missed.

It is usually done as spring is turning to summer and often under the glare of the sun, and it is a job that cannot be hurried. It is a lonely job too, and concentrated work. You cannot allow your attention to wander or your hoe will wander too. Random decapitation of the neat rows of plants is not the object of the exercise. It sets its own pace and if you hurry at it, it will tame you. Old boys tell tales of endless days, weeks even, with a hoe, working slowly along row after row. But if you have patience (and Busky had plenty of it), chopping out mangels can be a relaxation in itself.

Then there was Jean. Jean's tasks of cooking and clean-ing, though far removed from the vital business of work-ing the soil and shoeing the horses, hold the farm together and keep it at work. I certainly would not have been able to do as much work without her sustenance. She would often take pity on me when she spied from the kitchen window that my strength was flagging as I slung forkfuls of muck. The kitchen window would ease open a little, and out would pop a mug of hot tea. On rainy days I might go into the kitchen just to inhale the smell of that night's supper. 'That smells so good, I might have a bowl of it before I go, Jean,' I might suggest.

'You won't,' was her sharp reply. 'That's for the dogs!' Man *and* beast are well fed at Weylands Farm.

'Jean's father was a wonder with ferrets,' Roger said once during one of our after-dinner sessions round the kitchen table. 'I had a ferret escape the other day and Jean ran after it and caught it. There was a customer in the forge. He said to her, "Aren't you afraid?" She said, "Afraid? I did nothing else with my father all winter."'

'He'd come home,' Roger continued, 'after a day's rabbiting with those ferrets, and you wouldn't be able to see his bike for rabbits. His biggest catch was 2,100 in twenty-two days. They were all packed in hampers and sent to London.'

Roger had a way of stopping a tale in such a way that it was clear that more was to follow. So no one spoke.

'He used to eat fat pork and a raw onion for his breakfast,' Roger beamed. 'Grand old boy, he was, grand old boy.'

And where are the grand old boys of tomorrow? Probably lurking around Weylands Farm, building up a store of knowledge and wisdom which in their later years they will be able to dispense freely or keep to themselves, as the mood happens to take them. The line is continuing, all right. There was Stuart, a former apprentice of Roger's who now has his diploma and so is second in command in the forge. And there's the 'boy' Fred, an apprentice farrier and the son of a former apprentice of Roger's. It would be difficult to find a better school than the one that Roger Clark runs beneath the tin roof of his forge; he has won every major prize for the shoeing of heavy horses that anybody has bothered to present, and has much wisdom to hand on.

Apprentices here learn about more than the feet of

hunters and children's ponies. They will work the Suffolk horses on the fields, help with thrashing, potato-planting and any job that needs to be done to keep the farm going. An apprenticeship here covers a broad canvas. I asked Roger what happens if apprentices didn't care for it. 'They adapt, or they don't seem to last long.'

If I envied any one of them, it was the 'boy' Robert. Now, he really *is* a boy, only ten. Every day after school he would come running up the lane in search of a job to do with horses. 'When I grow up,' I heard him say, breathlessly, 'I want to be a colt-breaker, like Cheryl.'

'It's a funny story, really,' said Cheryl. 'Every year we take a horse and cart to the Spring Market at Stoke-by-Nayland. It's to raise money for the church, run by Lady Rowley.'

'Well, one year,' Roger butted in, 'I gave this little boy a ride on the cart. He was only three, and do you know what he said? He said, "When I grow up, I am going to work with Suffolk Punches." Three years old!'

And that was young Robert. Seven years later, he seems well on his way to achieving his ambition. I watched him carefully, and noted the confident way he approached the horses and the attention with which he hung on to everything that Roger or Cheryl told him. If ever there was a horseman in the making, he is one.

# Eleven

'YOU *will* have a pair of clean smart trousers, and a shirt and tie, *and* a bowler hat,' and Cheryl banged her fist on the tea table to emphasise every order. 'And you *will* be here at five-thirty in the morning.' And she nearly split her sides laughing at the thought of my turning out at what was a reasonable hour for her but an unlikely time of day for me to be up.

Cheryl was not a lady who often gave orders with such force that they rattled the cutlery on the table, but this was *her* time of year; the gruelling months of winter had been but a preparation for the long summer days when she could load her beloved horses into a lorry and flee to agricultural and county shows in all corners of the country. I remember her telling me how she would be quite happy to spend the whole summer in the cab of her lorry, and how Roger groaned at the prospect.

'I don't like going much further than Ipswich [fifteen miles away],' he muttered.

'And I have a job to get him that far sometimes,' added Cheryl.

But the showing of the horses, either as individuals standing alone and being judged for their looks, or dressed in a glittering harness of brass and rich black leather, was not an idle pastime for the Clarks. It was a business just as serious as running a farm, and approached with due solemnity. Cheryl Clark is very much into winning. She was a champion athlete at school, representing England, and insists, 'If you're not up there winning you might as well not bother.'

Hence my orders for the Woodbridge Horse Show: clean trousers, shirt and an early rise.

'Don't forget, half past five,' Cheryl roared again, and laughed some more, clearly expecting me to be unable to be conscious at such an hour. It hardened my resolve.

That night I ironed shirts, pressed trousers, looked for an old black bowler hat that I had bought for seven pounds in a junk shop in anticipation of the day when I would have to slip into the county show-goer's uniform of tweed and bowler hat. I set the alarm for half-past four and hardly slept a wink, waking every thirty minutes to check that I was not going to miss this appointment.

I was at Weylands Farm five minutes early and when I met Cheryl in the yard I ostentatiously looked at my watch, but she didn't rise to the bait. It would have been nice, just for once, to catch them out – to be up and about before them, to arrive at the farm and find them all soundly asleep and have had the horses fed and watered before they had stirred in their beds, but it was an imposs ible dream. Whatever time I arrived, at whatever time of year, they were at work and had been for some time.

But there was a concentrated silence about this morning's activity; partly because of the nature of the work and partly because Roger still looked in need of another hour or two's sleep. He was standing on a wobbly stool beside Richard, whose turn it was to go to the show, together with Thomas. From his balancing position, Roger was taking handfuls of Thomas's mane and plaiting into it three thick strands of raffia tied in a knot at one end:

'bass', it is called. Every six inches or so, into the plaiting he would fix strands of red and yellow ribbon which were held flying by twisted pieces of wire. It is called 'braiding' and is traditional and highly skilled. It was the way the Suffolk horse had been presented in the show-ring for as long as horse shows had been held, but in the dim light of the barn and with an early-morning weariness in your eyes, that didn't make the fiddly nature of it any easier to be patient with.

'You can use these,' said Roger, holding up a ribbon he was about to work into the plaiting, 'to make your horse look just that bit better. If its old neck isn't quite as strong as you'd like it to be, you can make the ribbons in the middle stick up just that bit longer than the ones at either end, and that will give a bit more curve to his neck when the judge first spots him.'

I wandered outside to where Cheryl was plaiting a similar bunch of raffia, this time into Thomas's tail. 'Do you usually do tails?' I asked.

'Roger does manes because there's less work in manes. If there were less work in tails Roger would do tails!' and her nimble fingers grabbed another strand or two of hair and wove them in and out of the raffia, resulting in a spectacular pattern down the length of the tail. No amount of close inspection would ever reveal the secret of how it was done.

'The only way is to do it over and over again. I started with a tail off a dead horse that someone gave me, and I just did it and did it till I got it right. You can't rush it, you'll never do it,' and she winced as she pulled tight the last knot that held the whole sculpture in place, the steely horse hairs cutting into her fingers as she pulled. The tail was tight as a parcel, as intricately woven as a Persian rug;

and it was not yet quarter to six.

Roger was still on his braiding stool in the barn. Cheryl disappeared into the house. The occasional distant crash of the frying-pan hinted at breakfast.

'I sometimes wish I'd stuck with Shire horses. We had Shires before we ever had Suffolks,' Roger admitted in a weary sort of way. 'There's big money in Shires, there's nothing in Suffolks. We've won the best team of heavy horses at the Royal Show three years on the trot – that's never been known before. If we'd had as much success with Shires as we've had with Suffolks, our team might be worth twenty thousand quid. But Suffolks will never be worth that much. Just because you've got a champion Suffolk horse doesn't mean it's worth a penny more than if it was just standing in a field.'

I gave Richard a morale-building pat, out of Roger's sight.

Roger, of course, was right. The decline of the Suffolk horse has been spectacular. From the days when it had been the workhorse of the most productive parts of arable England to its near-extinction in the 1960s, its numbers have rallied a little of late, but when I asked Roger how many full teams of Suffolk horses there were now, he answered, 'Only one, and they're all in this barn.' And we went to breakfast.

I have not said much about breakfast at Weylands Farm until now because it took some time for me to realise how fundamental breakfast was to being able to do one's day's work. On normal working days, I would have watered and mucked out and groomed for an hour before eating, and having been up a good hour before that, I was more than ready for the eight o'clock call. It was what you would call a good 'working' breakfast. Fried eggs, bacon, sausages, sometimes tomatoes and hefty chunks of toast. Roger often cures his own bacon, using an old recipe involving salt and beer and much else, and there was a good chance that the porky sausages had been grunting and waddling their way round his fields the year before. The eggs, yolks always incandescent yellow, were by courtesy of the rabble of hens that clucked around the yard, and the whole masterpiece was orchestrated by Cheryl into a sumptuous feast that kept a working man well fuelled for a good five hours. Muesli-and-dry-toast-eaters might wear a smile of self-satisfaction at the thought of their low-fat, low-protein diet compared with the high-fat, high-cholesterol feast at Weylands but try following a plough for five hours on a bellyful of nuts and skimmed milk, and I swear you would shortly be stuffing Cheryl's sausages down you as if they were the very source of life.

'What time's that show start, then?' Cheryl asked, idly.

'It's always ten o'clock,' said Roger. More toast was offered.

'Are you sure,' said Cheryl, casually.

'Y'p,' repeated Roger, 'always ten o'clock.' I thanked them for breakfast and went into the yard to brush a few more horses.

Ten minutes later there was a shriek. Doors banged. Dogs started to yap. Horses became uneasy and shifted from foot to foot. In the distance a lorry engine churned into life. Hens scattered. The show, they had just discovered, started at nine. The Clarks were late. The Clarks were *never* late. Things started to move quickly.

Cheryl thundered down the drive with her lorry. A huge converted furniture van, it had been painted in appropriate battle grey. Above the cab, a sign proudly boasted 'SUFFOLK HORSES'. The ramp was dropped, and with an electric winch two tons of four-wheel dray (a bright-red and highly polished vehicle for the show-ring) was hauled in, quickly followed by Richard and Thomas, who were bundled into the lorry so rapidly that they cannot have known whether they were coming or going.

The gears crunched and Cheryl Clark was, with more haste than she had anticipated, on the road for another season.

Roger and I followed in a car.

The atmosphere among visitors to the Woodbridge Horse Show, or at least among the Suffolk Punch owners (who are somewhat overshadowed, but only in terms of numbers, by gymkhana pony kids and tense show-jumpers), is one of fierce competition alternating with touching comradeship. All Suffolk-owners know all the other owners, there are no secrets between them, and they know who the real competition is, and who can be discarded. They will rally to help anyone who might have broken a bridle, burst a lorry tyre, forgotten a bale of hay; but in the ring it is a battle for supremacy. And then it's all a laugh again as soon as the judging is over.

Our horses were ready to go into the ring; others were still being brushed. Worried exhibitors were anxiously scanning the field for a groom who might help with the final bit of braiding or adjust a ribbon in a forelock. And then, without any visible signal being made, the horses made their way to the ring. For animals bred from the same line (and all Suffolk horses can be traced back to one famous stallion: Crisp's Horse of Ufford, foaled in 1768), they are remarkably different. Some are much richer and browner; others have almost blonde manes. Some are small, and might at first glance be mistaken for overweight light horses; some are muscular and vast, powerful enough to haul the world off its axis. Some are just fat; others bulge with muscles that make heavyweight boxers look skinny and puny by comparison. As they parade to the ring, the lightweight hunters and jumpers edge backwards, being careful not to pick any fights with these giants.

And how do you pick one as being better than the other? What is the right shape for a Suffolk horse? There have to be as many opinions as there are owners.

'Look at that thing,' whispered Roger. 'No more than a cripple, that ain't.' I could not see what he meant. 'Damned miserable-looking horse over there,' he went on. But it looked a jolly old chap to me. I did not have the eye. I suggested to Roger that 'that looks a good 'un'. 'Too long in the body,' he would say. 'But he's got a good neck,' I'd reply. 'Yeah, but no leg,' Roger would add. But their owners loved them, proudly walked them round the ring and then ran with them as they trotted so that the judge could see every muscle flex and watch every footfall.

Thomas won his class. Best Suffolk gelding – Cheryl beamed as she stalked from the ring, the huge horse towering over his short but bursting-with-pride owner. One more winner's rosette to add to the hundreds. The Clarks win a lot. Other competitors don't talk of winning a class of geldings; that is not always their ambition. To 'beat the Clarks' would be enough.

Roger and I went to watch the next class: stallions, founders of the next generation of Suffolk Punches.

'Years ago, some of these horses would never have been anywhere near a ring. Look at 'em. Half of 'em should be shot.' This is not bad sportsmanship, but the perception of the most successful exhibitor of Suffolk horses of his generation. 'They're getting too small these days. Like bloody ponies, more often than not. How are we supposed to breed big upstanding geldings that we can come out and beat Shires with, as we've done in the past, with bloody ponies like these!'

'Thomas did well,' I added after a suitable pause.

'Yeah, that old horse did, you know. He's six now, but when he was about three I thought he was never going to make it. I nearly 'ad 'im shot, as well!' He laughed.

Behind us, the grey battle lorry was revving up. Sheep, cattle and the other horses were at home waiting to be fed, and everyone's breakfast was beginning to wear off.

# Twelve

THE winning of silver cups at county shows was the only glimmer of light in an otherwise dank and miserable summer. I had always believed that farmers moaned about the weather because moaning came naturally to them, but this year, with its torrential rains, late spring and early frosts, was a year that was only fit for spitting out. The shows were the only pastime, the only thing to do while everyone waited for their corn to ripen and tried to put to the back of their minds the thought that in such an appalling summer as this it might never do so.

Roger and I found another way of filling the odd hour when there was either no work to do on the farm or what work there was could be left at the slightest excuse. We went to 'farm sales'.

These are auctions held after a farmer has either sold up, or gone out of cattle into corn, or out of corn into liquidation. Some were of greater interest to us than others. Combine-harvesters and tractors had little appeal, but a careful reading between the lines of the auctioneers' catalogues might reveal pieces of harness for sale, or an old cart or 'assorted bygones', to use the phrase much loved by these catalogue-writers. Of course, what might be bygones to them are the essential daily equipment at Weylands Farm, and so if there was ever a hint of some rich and aged pickings, we would be into the car and off.

I remember a hefty catalogue thumping on to the doormat, sent by a Cambridge auctioneer. Even page one had the saliva swirling in my mouth. Lot 1, 'a collection of rural bygones', held a wealth of East Anglian promise. Then came a 'cart-horse collar – 25″': a decent-sized collar for a Suffolk Punch – anything less than twenty-five inches would be too small. 'A corn chandler's desk, a Bentall Eclipse root-slicer, a Ransomes "Double Tom" potato-ridger, a Cottis Epping adjustable inter-row horse hoe, a tumbril cart, a Massey Harris two-horse sail-reaper . . .' and the crowning glory of all, a magnificence of wooden and iron engineering: 'A Ransomes, Sims and Jeffries Model AM54 – 54″ threshing drum with self-feed, built on iron spoke wheels, serial number 59311.' There were also steam ploughing engines and vintage tractors, but these did not catch our eye in any way.

I suppose, if you are a regular reader of auctioneers' catalogues, you are prepared to be disappointed by the discrepancy between what you think you have read and what appears before your eyes when you get there. Roger and I were on the field where the sale was to be held nice and early. Not quite as early as we had planned, as the truck had a flat tyre and, in his farrier's way, Roger sent it over to the garage to have its 'near hind' tyre fixed. When we eventually arrived, the machinery was lying on the grass, while harness and 'bygones' were in a barn. I strode over to the 'bygones'. True enough, they were indeed aged artefacts, but it was difficult to see how a box containing an old cycle lamp, a jamjar with a paint brush in it and some rusty odds and ends was even worth an auctioneer lifting his hammer.

The harness was even more disappointing. Sure enough,

there were heavy horse collars, but most had more straw poking out of them than sound leather to hold the straw in place. Some piles of harness just crumbled to dust as you picked them up. At one time, they would have been oiled and cleaned with loving care, but when the tractors finally arrived on the farms, the collars were hung on the old stable walls and forgotten about. I have read tales of men in tears the day the horses were sold to make way for the machines. That any of it survives is a small miracle.

Roger, with the eye of an experienced hunter after treasures, knew that a little digging would be well rewarded. He ferreted through bridles and found one with an interesting bit, or another that could only ever have been used in the North Country. He identified a stallion harness and told me how the straps on it were for holding a rug to throw over the horse to keep the chill wind off, and the other was for a sleeping roll for the man who toured the stallion around the county. Within half an hour, Roger had quickly determined what was worth anything, and what was 'worth nowt'.

Then the bidding began. There was little shouting and no waving of catalogues in the air, but there was an intensity matched only by that of the fine-art auctions, especially when the bidding broke the £50 barrier – which wasn't very often. Some of the bidders were old farmers in raincoats and flat caps, while some were enthusiasts and collectors who were mostly interested in the old tractors and went into corners and spoke passionately about 1936 carburettors. There were a few people that I recognised from the Suffolk Horse Society dinner. They had all been looking at the harness, and collars and carts.

And then there were the antique-dealers – vermin amongst the genuine hunters. They spoilt the fun for everyone by pushing prices up to dizzy heights like £30, when everyone knew the item in question was worth a tenner at the most. They were the ones who stood at the back of the room, Parker pen in hand, scribbling prices in the margins of the catalogue. Nor did I take kindly to the souvenir-hunters. I spotted a man standing over a particularly fine leather collar with a tape-measure in his hand, checking it this way and that. I asked him what sort of horse he had, did he work it, would the collar fit?

'Horse, mate? No, I haven't got a bloody horse. I've got a bistro in Camberley. I thought this would look nice on the wall. I was just seeing whether it fitted.' It did, and so he paid more than it was worth, and probably deprived a horse of it. He certainly deprived Roger of it.

Roger had been strangely quiet so far. He hadn't bid for much, and it was only the slightest flick of his hand that gave the game away. But what was he bidding for? What lot number were we up to? I watched his wrist flick again, and we were up to ten pounds. He went even further. He stayed in as it went past fifteen and didn't stop till it had been knocked down to him at nineteen whole pounds.

'Did I get it?' asked Roger, not certain or caring too much whether the hammer had fallen in his favour or someone else's. Being assured that it was his, he wandered over to survey his new treasure. Lot 93 – 'three wooden pigeon-hole storage racks'!

'But whatever use are those?' I asked, hardly believing that anyone could find a use for three sets of shelving that looked as though they had been ripped none too carefully from the letter-sorting compartment of an old mail train.

'I just fancied 'em. A damned useful lot, I would say. Very useful indeed.'

And so were the spiky chain harrows, and other heaps

of rusty metallic odds and ends that we eventually heaped into the trailer and restored to their rightful position on a working farm. Except for the pigeon-hole shelves.

'We'll put 'em in the barn. Very useful they will be, one day.'

What a great day out, and a cheap one too, where you can stand and gasp at the silly prices that people pay, or enjoy the skirmish between rival bidders. Somewhat bitten by this acquisitive bug, I scanned the local newspaper for the next farm sale, and hoped it would be soon.

# Thirteen

GERRY'S departure meant that new, heavy responsibilities fell upon my inexperienced shoulders. It was all very well to have charge of a horse knowing that a man with forty years' experience was just round the corner to get you out of any trouble; it was another to be told to get a horse into plough chains and bring him down to such and such a field, knowing that every step it took was a direct consequence of your actions. I felt sure that in my muddled efforts I would miss some vital link of either leather or chain which would mean that the long trudge to the field would soon be followed by a hasty and shaming sprint back to the harness-room. I remember thinking that the plough line would be an easy thing to forget. Because it is neither made of leather, nor jangles like chain, it would be easy to leave it behind in the rush to collar-up and get to work. But to turn up on a field with a pair of harnessed horses and no plough line was as much use as building a fire and forgetting the match. So I checked, and checked again, every time.

In the middle of May, on a dullish but mild afternoon, Roger and I went to sow kale. When it was fully grown it would be green and leafy and provide winter feed for sheep, who would pass the chilly days gnawing the last bit of succulence from its stems.

'That's a Smyth drill. Best seed drill ever made,' Roger

said, as he heaved the tarpaulin off yet another of these aged and highly complicated contraptions made of wood, iron and heavy chains. Like all farm machinery of its age (1930s and '40s), it was built to the sort of design a child might conjure up with a Meccano set. It was obvious engineering. If you wished a wheel to turn, you connected it with a chain to another wheel that was already turning. If that meant a bend through ninety degrees by a flailing chain running the whole length of the machine and back again, so be it. It was the effect that was required, and the means were of little import.

'You can do very precise work with a Smyth drill,' said Roger, as he tipped the fine kale seeds into the hopper. Rupert, one of the oldest horses in the stable, was between the shafts. He was a grand old horse, veteran of many a winter's ploughing and spring sowing. He creaked a little and wheezed a bit, but that was the only clue to his fourteen years – that and the privileges that his age had brought him, such as being allowed to make his own way into the barn. He needed no leading, just the field gate opening and he would find his own way to his stall. I was startled one day to find a Suffolk wandering around the yard untethered. 'Horse free!' I shouted, and ran forward to capture him before he made a break for it. But it was only old Rupert. He was such a gentle old soul that after his lone ambles to the stalls, no one would remember to clip on his tether. When that happened, it was his practice to walk around the yard 'sunning hisself', as Cheryl described it.

The kale seed was as fine and as black as lead shot, and it was my job to follow behind Roger, who steered the machine, and watch carefully to see that seed was falling freely into the ground and not getting stuck in its travels through the innards of the contraption. It was easy when the sun was upon it; the fine black seed sparkled and glistened as it dropped on to the dry earth, but when we reached the end of the field and returned in the opposite direction, the sun behind it made it impossible to see. I often called for a halt for no good reason.

'Now,' Roger said as he got to the edge of the field after the first pass with the drill, 'help me unhook that chain, and at the same time pull the horse round so we're heading in the opposite direction.' I got into the rhythm: pull on the lines to the bit, and bring the horse's head round just as the chain becomes free. Roger attached the chain on the other side and we were swiftly heading in the opposite direction with the grace of a windjammer tacking through the eye of the wind. Most times, anyway. Sometimes I would pull Rupert into too tight a turn and we would have to back and fill like a learner driver first attempting a three-point turn. Sometimes, Rupert just went his own way and under my breath I would mutter, 'Lousy old hoss.'

But Roger cursed too. He hated 'short work'. Few fields have square corners and so you end up with an odd-shaped triangle of land where the passes get shorter and more irritating the nearer you get to the corner. It means that the very end of the whole job becomes the slowest part, and a last-minute spurt of energy to get the damned job finished is bound to be thwarted as the turns get tighter and more frequent. But within the hour, the job was done. Roger headed for the forge to shoe a horse and, much to my surprise, said, 'Put Rupert in that flat roller and just roll that all flat. Up and down and then once or twice round the headland.' And he was off.

This was a turning point. This was the first time I had

been trusted, alone, with a horse, in a field with a real job of work to do. It might not have been the most vital job on the farm, but it had to be done. It was real work, it mattered. Straight lines were paramount, especially as the field was in full view of the approach to the farm and any irregularities would surely be remarked upon.

I led Rupert the length of the field, dragging the roller behind, muttering words of encouragement as we went. At the end I looked back. The flattened earth we had just rolled made a weaving wandering path. A crippled drunk could have walked straighter. As the outside edge would be part of the headland, I could smooth that out with the final circuit of the roller, but as for the other edge, I would have to overlap and try to do better the next time. So off we trundled in the other direction.

The field was on a hillside and the roller slid, so instead of rolling a path of land parallel to the first, we ended up with a wedge ending in what was almost a point. So that had to be overlapped. It became clear that if each strip was to be corrected like this, it was going to take at least three or four times as long as it should. These deep thoughts occupied my mind to the extent that Rupert's meanderings went unnoticed by me, and unchecked, and our next rolled path had an outline like the blade of an abused bread-knife.

It wasn't till the next pass of the roller that I discovered the solution to all my problems. It was quite simple really; all I had to do was let Rupert get on with the job. I had been *driving* him, whereas he only needed *leading*. Instead of guiding every one of his footfalls, all I needed to do was to set him in the right direction and offer an occasional correction. When it came to the business of walking in a straight line, Rupert had far more experience than

I did. This discovery having been made, I went back to the top of the field and started again, glancing over my shoulder to check that Roger and Cheryl were not watching and thoroughly enjoying themselves at my expense.

When the job was finished, I proudly unhitched Rupert from the roller and walked him back to the barn, rehearsing as I walked what had to be done to put the horse away properly so that the next time I came to the farm an irate Cheryl would not be waiting with a stinging scolding on her lips. I had to unhook the bit from Rupert's mouth . . . let him drink water . . . walk him to the barn . . . take off the harness. Second nature to the Clarks, routine to be learned for me.

I looked behind me to see the results of the afternoon's labours on the rolled field. I could see only the kinks, the waverings of the roller and even an odd triangle of unrolled land. It looked worse as the sun sank and threw crazy shadows which emphasised every undulation. But a true artist is always the most critical of his work, so I hoped it didn't look too bad to a casual observer's eye. Back in the house, over a cup of tea, Cheryl asked Roger which horse I'd been using. Roger told her it was Rupert.

'Rupert,' she muttered. 'Hoss could have done that on his own!'

Talk about deflating what little pride a chap had left with one swift blow. It was enough to have any man diving into the deepest bottoms of his jacket pockets for a fag end.

# Fourteen

CHERYL was hardly to be seen on the farm during late June and early July. It was one county show after the next, and if her infrequent days at home didn't happen to coincide with one of my weekly visits to Weylands Farm, our two ships would pass in the night. We got regular reports back from all corners of the kingdom. We heard of a win here, a reserve championship there. Curses about judges, praise for others. There were moans about the muddy fields, and the sodden showgrounds where Cheryl and her mighty lorry had to set up camp. But the underlying theme of the year was success.

The upshot of it was that Roger had to make the breakfast. And quite skilled he became at it. His fried egg did not have the composure of one that might have come from Cheryl's pan, but the rest of it couldn't be faulted. I found Roger deep in study one morning, hardly speaking a word. He was peering intently into some veterinary tome. Animal science was one of Roger's abiding interests, and the kitchen was often sprinkled with veterinary textbooks, most of which dated from earlier this century. 'That's very interesting,' he would say and pause for another mouthful of bacon. This morning his mind was on cows, and in particular on twin calves that the old Red Poll cow had calved the day before (which explained the afterbirth that was lying around the yard).

'Twin calves can't go on to mate and produce a calf . . .' and he went into a detailed genetic explanation of how and why. I chewed a little more slowly on the bacon. There was a dead drake lying in the yard as well that morning. The balance of nature was much in evidence.

Major was poorly too.

'Look at his old legs, blown up they are,' and Roger pointed to the puffy limbs of the newest horse to come to the farm. He was a darker Suffolk than most, not as heavy as the others, and clearly not well.

'Needs a good physic. I reckon that's constipation,' and Roger took out a packet of 'physic balls'. The label promised swift remedial action for all manner of animal ills - all thanks to a recipe that had been formulated more than a century ago. Roger handed one to me to feel. It was almost black, and a bit spongy, smaller than a ping-pong ball but bigger than a gob-stopper; with no hesitation, Roger took one in his hand, opened the horse's mouth wide by inserting his thumb into the corner and then put his entire arm, almost up to the elbow, into the horse's mouth. When he had reached as far into the deeper recesses of the throat as he felt able to go, he deposited the physic ball, quickly withdrew his arm, and winced.

'That's the only problem. They sometimes bite you,' he said, modestly for a man whose arm could easily have been removed by one snap from this animal. He then watched the horse's throat intently from the top of its neck down to its stomach to watch for the bulge of the ball making its way down the gullet to the stomach. Nothing. No visible ripple.

'They can hang on to them for ages.' Major gulped and Roger took his hand away. But Roger was not convinced, and rightly too, for no sooner had Major turned his head than he spat the thing out into his manger.

Roger called for reinforcements. He took an iron rod, the length of a poker, with a recess on the end which took the physic ball. He opened the horse's mouth again and, instead of his hand, plunged the poker to the back of Major's mouth. That did the trick. A huge lump could clearly be seen working its way down his throat. Laxative relief would soon be at hand for old Major.

Again that afternoon there was a job for me to do; more of the responsibility from which I was beginning to derive deep pleasure. I took Prince up to the potato field with orders to earth up the rows of spuds. The green leaf was high now, and as the potatoes grew they had to be covered with earth to make room for more to come, and to ensure that the light didn't get through to those near the surface and turn them green. I had help this time, from a chap called Ian who had been given a job after the departure of Lynn, the stable girl. Ian seemed a keen chap, and an ideal man to have helping. Especially as it put me in a position of knowing something that someone else didn't – a rare state of affairs for me. We hitched Prince to the same double-sided plough that had originally carved the trench into which we had set the potato seed a couple of months before, but this time, instead of driving it along the rows, we drove it between them so that the earth piled up around the stems, leaving a deep and clean furrow between them.

Ian led the horse, and I steered the plough with enormous pride, bursting like a child who is allowed for the very first time to hold one of his father's precious tools or carry his mother's shopping. It was not as skilled as ploughing, since the furrow already existed and we were simply deepening it, but I was in charge of the horse, responsible for getting the job done, and wanted to 'do it right'.

The ability and intelligence of the Suffolk horse is remarkable and, to a beginner like me, reassuring. Prince was able to walk the length of the furrow, between the growing potatoes, and when he was done you might never guess that he had passed that way, so sure and careful was every footfall. As we went along, I learned to press on to the plough handles to drive it deeper when the ground got harder, and ease off when we hit a sandier or less stony patch. We did two or three lengths of the field and Ian was clearly itching to have a go. So I led Prince, while he took the handles and I was able to offer advice and encouragement. I had surely come a long way in less than six months. I had also come to the point where the day's work ended when the day's work was done, and not when the hands of the clock arrived at some arbitrary point. So I ploughed on, well after the time I would usually leave, and set off for home quite content.


Midsummer. The most false of all fixed points in the calendar, for it is rare to have had any summer by midsummer's day and it is the cruellest of planetary tricks to start the shortening of the days before we have had a chance to feel the full warmth of the sun – especially in a year when there had been more rain than anyone could remember.

I took an evening stroll round Weylands Farm on midsummer's night, which fell on a Sunday. It was not a scene that would have roused Constable to take up his palette or inflamed a poet to verse. It was damp, and humid, not warm and summery. The midges didn't even bother to fly.

But memories cut through the dank, hazy gloom. This was my halfway point in the year, and I had had time to store up reminiscences. I had served half my time. I was on the homeward stretch. And the thought saddened me, for I had come to adore this place despite its frustrations and exertions.

The muck-heap, on the left as I drove up the farm, had taken on a new shape and texture since the winter days when I had piled it high with hot steaming straw from the yard. It had shrunk as biological changes within this natural reactor had reduced the mucky, strawy mass to rich manure. The top of the heap was dry now, earthy in colour, and of course the steam no longer rose.

The field of kale where I had followed the Smyth drill for the first time was now green and bursting into succulent leaf, eventually to feed fattening lambs that were still with their mothers. It was the field I had rolled, and rolled again, and again, till the lines were straight. There was no hint of my undulations now. Just green leaf.

Thomas and Toby, the young Punches, grazed the next field. They leaped around as I approached, full of life, seeming to forget for a moment that they each had a ton of themselves to fling around. Thomas was generally reckoned to be the finest Suffolk gelding of his time, and I think he knew it.

I wandered down into the valley to find a field of beans in white fragrant flower. They grew like broad beans in a garden but would not be harvested till almost black, and ready to be crushed and fed to cattle. The last time I had been here I ended up a muddy disconsolate figure, having endured a bitter day behind two young horses, with Gerry in an uncompromising mood, and an equally chilly plough in my hands. It was here that Richard 'swoundered 'isself' and collapsed through lack of air, here that the grumpy Gerry had flung the full weight of the plough against my leg as he swung it round at the end of the furrow. I put my hand on my thigh to see if the pain was still there. But it had gone. All there was to show for it was row after row of beans.

The field of oats already stood high and waved in the breeze. That too had been blank earth the last time I had worked on it; and Wheeping Hills, the highest of the fields on the farm, where I had first put hand to plough six months before, was bursting with young barley crying out for sun and warmth.

All was quiet by the time I got back to the yard. It must have been nine o'clock. Some horses had gone to boxes for the night, while others stood and licked along the empty mangers for the umpteenth time in search of the smallest of grains that they might have missed. The geese didn't even bother to hiss, the dogs didn't raise a bark. Instead they just looked, the horses too, and I took a long hard look back. Halfway.

When Cheryl's travelling circus of Suffolk Punches found themselves on parade close to home, I became involved. I didn't have the skills of grooming or braiding to be much use at the big county shows, or even at the mighty Royal, but I had a pair of hands, a little experience by now and a willingness to get a kettle to the boil in the cavernous horse-lorry and cart mugs of tea round stables whilst others brushed and combed and plaited.

The Suffolk Show was one such occasion. Because it was *the* county show and these were the county's own

111

horses, there seemed to be even more concentration in the air, tinier details to attend to, even more horses to bring up to parade standard. The horses must have sensed it too, for they found rich and tasty clover hay, or 'stover', in their haynets rather than the usual ration of dried meadow grass.

It didn't rain on Suffolk Show day. In a summer such as this was, that is an event worth recording in itself. It meant that the hours of preparation were not wasted, for there must be no more cruel fate than to have the harness and horses on which one might have been sweating for days before the show reduced to a soggy and lacklustre mass. Not only the horses, but sheep and cattle too! If you have only groomed horses it can come as a shock to groom a lumpy and bony cow, as I was asked to do. Cows are not natural show-offs. Whereas a horse will take positive pleasure from the rough stroke of the brush, cows can clearly see no point in it. Roger sent me with a serrated rubber scrubbing brush to try and get some shine on to his Red Poll cow. I was told to tie the cow up with a short scope, for they don't seem to like freedom much. It has to be all or nothing: either the freedom to wander as far as they wish, or else to be tied to the wall on a mere inch of rope. In this restrained position the old cow rolled her eye so that she got a full picture of what was happening behind her. The old girl looked a bit wild as more and more white of eye appeared, and she froze as I picked up the brush, her eyes as white as glaciers by now.

It was like taking a brush to a bag of bones. Lumpy bits stuck out from places that seemed odd to me compared with the regular and predictable muscular feel of a horse. It was easy to rub too hard, as well, and leave bald patches. But when grooming sheep, the reverse was true.

No amount of rubbing seemed to have the slightest effect. Roger even told me to use a bit of sandpaper on the black bits of the ram's face, to get the few white hairs out of it. Unlike the cow, the ram was brought into show condition by being given a skilful shearing, a thoroughly good wash and a quick oiling of its black head to give it an eye-catching shine. Whether it won a prize or not was then down to its breeding and its feeding. How judges, faced with thirty sheep in a ring, can spot one from another and declare one to be a better shape than its neighbour is beyond me.

There was satisfaction in having the cow, the sheep and the horses together at the Suffolk Show, for these particular three Suffolk breeds of farm animal are known as the 'Trinity': the Suffolk horse, the Suffolk sheep and the rich red cow they call the Red Poll. The Red Poll is becoming as rare as the Suffolk horse, but like her equine partner in this agricultural triangle she was once the mainstay of many small family farms. She was a 'good milker', and a good beef animal too; she was what they called a 'farmer's cow'. An all-rounder, who has now been displaced by specialist animals that may be either better milkers or better meat producers. Modern farmers like their animals to concentrate on one thing at a time, and the multi-talented Red Poll seems to have had its day.

While the pace of a farming day might be active but measured, the feel of the county show day is much more one of tedium punctuated with panic. If your horses are due in the ring at, say, ten-thirty, the hours between seven and eight will drag. You might be brushing, but in a measured sort of way, believing that you have all the time in the world. As soon as the clock has turned nine, however, the next sixty minutes will drain away as if a tap

113

had been opened. When you exhibit as many horses as the Clarks, with some in harness, others in either a pair, four- or six-horse team, there are enough of these panic points during any typical show day for complete exhaustion to have set in well before lunchtime.

During a typical hiatus, Cheryl turned to Roger and said, 'Who's going to drive the dust-cart?'

'What dust-cart?' replied Roger, nonplussed.

What Cheryl had remembered, and the others had forgotten in the rush to get horses in the ring, was the parade of working horses that was a feature new to the Suffolk Show. It was a feature new to any show, come to that. It was an attempt by the 'few' to prove to the 'many' that there was still a place for the working horse on the farm. All manner of breeds of heavy horses were represented; Clydesdales, Suffolks, Shires and a north European heavy called the Ardenne were to parade around the showring, blatantly cocking a snook at the 'advanced' machinery that overshadowed the rest of the showground.

Prince, one of my old friends from the early muck-carting days, was booked to pull the Manchester Corporation dust-cart. It was, I understood, no antique vehicle but purpose-built for modern use and was regularly seen on the streets of the northern town. The message it was there to convey was quite simple: there is still work for horses to do in town or country!

'Paul can drive old Prince,' said Roger. My face froze in a questioning look. 'I don't know what it's like but it'll just be a bit of a flat cart with a few bins on the back,' he added.

'Yeah,' said Cheryl, 'just a few bins on the back. Take old Prince down at about two o'clock.'

And that was that. I had been volunteered.

114

Just before two, I put a bridle on the horse and led him out of his box. I must have led him out of the yard at the farm scores of times, but this time an unfamiliar animal was on the other end of the leading rein. It was still Prince in body, but what a transformation in mind and attitude. He threw his head around as we walked the length of the stables past all the other Suffolks. He broke into a gentle trot, and had to be firmly held back. Then he would see his way ahead clear, and make a headlong charge and all the while I would be bellowing, 'Steady on, old hoss . . . *steady!*'

Then we met the pipe band – almost the last straw. As each kilted Scotsman blew the first breath into the bag-pipes, the unfamiliar skirl had Prince running in circles with me on the end, tugging at his bit and hoping that his hyperactive feet didn't cripple some innocent bystander, or puncture the big bass drum. Having survived the band, despite a last-minute attempt by the tambourine-player to frighten the horse out of his skin, we made it to the ring where the dust-cart awaited.

I could describe it in many ways, but 'a bit of a flat cart with dustbins on' it was not! It was the size of a small furniture lorry. High off the ground, broad in the wheel-base, and built so that the driver could not in any way see behind him except by leaning dangerously far to one side, it looked like a monster to me. With help, I put Prince between the shafts, I jumped up on to the seat and told him to 'G'up'. With a mighty lurch he put his whole weight into the straining leather collar, and we moved off into the procession behind a man and two Shires who were hauling a grass-mowing machine.

Prince was keen. Too keen. Intoxicated by the showground atmosphere and heady on his rich feed, he

115

charged along, my arms having just sufficient strength to keep him at the walk and prevent him from going his own galloping way. He pulled and I pulled, a disastrous combination in horse and driver that can often end in tears. An hour in the showring had my arms aching like six hours of muck-carting. As I led Prince away, I caught sight of Roger with his four-horse team, heading for the ring. They looked full of themselves too. Roger's arms bulged, his face reddened a bit. But within five minutes, he'd have won his battle with them. They would be bending to his will, performing to his command, and the pulling match between horse and master would be over. But that's a horseman for you. I just ached.

# Fifteen

I HAD great expectations of the harvest. Surely this would be the golden time of the year. Acres of sun-kissed corn would lie before us as we took our horses and machinery to 'bring the harvest home'. It would be a time of hard work, but also of great joy as we reaped our laborious investment of the previous twelve months. I saw us quenching our thirsts on the headlands beneath a glaring sun, or rustling through the fields by the light of the harvest moon.

'Bringing in the sheaves, bringing in the sheaves,' began the old hymn my grandmother used to sing to me, my first musical memory. 'We shall come rejoicing bringing in the sheaves.'

'Bloody wet,' I overheard Roger say on the phone. 'The yard's as wet as if it were mid-winter.' This was true. At the end of July, you do not expect to have to wear wellington boots to take the horses to the field, or to have to tread warily through the yard to avoid ponds of rain-water. So we waited for the summer to come. We had had a tempting taste of hot sunny weather at the beginning of July, but not long enough nor hot enough to do much for the crops, which were already well behind. And when the weather reverted to what those irritating forecasters call 'unsettled', the prospect of harvesting looked more and more remote.

There was only one stroke of good luck for Roger during the whole of July, and sadly I was not there to see it, but I heard much about it. For once, the downpour of torrential rain was a blessing. Quite simply, the whole of East Anglia had become so sodden through repeated dowsings that no heavy machinery was able to get on to the land. Tractors were sinking to their axles, and heavy potato-harvesting machines did not even venture through the field gates since there was no chance of them ever getting as far as the spuds before the powerful suction of the land brought them to a halt.

Not one potato was harvested in East Anglia that week – until one bright merchant remembered Roger Clark and his modest acreage of new potatoes. A horse, he thought, might well be able to tread where no tractor would dare to go. He was right, and the call went out from Weylands Farm for an army of boys, girls and women to assemble to harvest the potatoes. A pair of horses were harnessed to a potato-lifter, a plough-like affair which is driven along and through the ridges, casting spuds to one side as it goes. The army moved up behind it with baskets, picking up what were to the Clarks spuds as rich as jewels.

'That was so wet,' one of the girls told me later, 'that the rain was running down the furrows like rivers of water.'

'Our hands were so black with mud we couldn't tell what were potatoes and what was mud at one stage,' another told me. 'We used to wash our hands in the water pouring off the field and struggle on.'

Three days they harvested. Not one day was dry. But they reaped a handsome harvest.

'I've paid half the rent on the farm for the year,' boasted Roger, 'with that little patch of spuds.'

The corn's misfortune had been the potato man's gain and if ever there was proof needed that there was still sense in running a 'mixed' farm, this was it.

The cuckoo is the first sign of spring, the swallow a portent of summer. And Gerry's return heralded the corn harvest. I looked twice, but there was his unmistakable shuffling figure, staggering across the yard as if he had never been away. I didn't know whether I was pleased to see him or not. I had enjoyed my fling of solo responsibility, and I knew that now the 'old warrior' had returned I would have to bend to his unalterable will.

Roger asked us to fetch the binder, a sure sign that harvest was on his mind.

I had never seen a binder but felt as familiar with it as if I had. It is always at the heart of any painting or photograph of harvest time made in the first half of this century. It has a large revolving wooden structure at the front, like a waterwheel without the sides, which feeds the uncut standing corn into the knife. The rest of the operation is vague, but the object is to produce sheaves of corn perfect enough to go straight on the altar for harvest festival. As we set off with Rupert to bring the machine from the barn where it was stored, I felt the day could not be far off when we would happily be 'bringing in the sheaves'.

Gerry and I rode on the hitch-cart, a rusty two-wheeled vehicle which is in effect a mechanical link between horse and machinery. Horses have only pulling power, and to transfer power from horse to machine requires the horse equivalent of a tow-bar. Hence the hitch-cart.

With Rupert between the shafts, we ambled down the

lane to the valley and turned sharp right into the drive. Gerry stopped in front of an old, black wooden building surrounded by nettles and thistles so high that it was not possible to see what might be on the other side of them. I held the horse while Gerry set off on an exploration through this jungle, hacking his way through and swearing as he went.

He was gone a good ten minutes before I heard a cry: 'All right, bring your hoss through.'

I headed Rupert, complete with hitch-cart, straight through the undergrowth. On the other side we found a machine – an amalgam of rods, gears, couplings, chains, canvas sheets, wooden sails and iron wheels which all seemed to run in opposite directions, so it was far from clear where you attached the horse and in which direction the thing would eventually go. We had to back Rupert and the hitch-cart precisely, until Gerry was just able to drop the connecting pin through the hole in the tow-bar of each vehicle, and since the binder was too heavy to shunt around, it required the horse to be in exactly the right position. If the horse budged as much as an inch, the vital connection could not be made. After about ten minutes of backing to and fro, tempers were getting a little frayed.

Rupert rose above it all and obligingly dropped back an inch, allowing Gerry to drive the pin home. We set off for Weylands Farm, where the mysterious and magical binder stood until the weather decided to turn in our favour.

In fact, the weather could not have been more contrary. The nights grew cold and crisp under clearing skies and northerly winds. Central parts of England were reported to have had ground frosts, and this was the first week in August! Torrential rain beat the land and the standing corn; acre after acre was flattened as if rolled by a massive weight. And still the binder stood there. It looked at one stage as if it might stay there for the rest of the winter, for as field after field was flattened Roger considered calling in a combine-harvester, the modern farming giant which cuts the corn, thrashes the grain from it and spews it out in one operation. A fraction of the work, but many times the cost of taking a couple of horses up the top of the hill.

If there had been no choice, the binder would have had to cut the lot, flattened or not. When that was the only implement that farmers could call upon to salvage corn from the field that might be their only income for the next twelve months, then the binder had to be made to cut the corn. Roger could have made it cut those fallen fields, but the effort would have been enormous. In the end the upholding of tradition has its price, a price that Roger could not afford. With the exception of the field of rye, which still stood tall and proud, a combine would harvest the rest. So the binder waited for the rye to be ready and the land to be drier.

I was brought up short one reasonably fine summer's day in mid-August. So far, all the work I had done had been a contribution to my own year on the farm. I had ploughed and sowed, and surely I would soon be reaping and mowing. The muck I had laboriously carted I would soon spread and help plough into the soil. The early-season ploughing of which I had had a taste was now smothered beneath a dense blanket of swaying, though unripe, barley. The seed I had sown was sprouting in all four corners of the farm, and would be cut and harvested well before my year was out.

So it was a surprise when Roger gathered the Suffolk

ewes into the yard to be put to the prize ram. This would bring forth lambs after Christmas, lambs that I might not see. In many ways, my farming year was detectably on the wane.

Suffolks look like sheep should, as a child would draw one. Black-faced, woolly and plump and, as Roger remarked after a typical chase round the yard, 'They can't run as fast as some of them mountain sheep. They're a bit easier to catch.'

It has also been said of sheep that they have one aim in life and that is to die no matter what you do. This was evident as we drove them into the yard with the help of Roger's two collies, who, by a combination of growling and stalking, did their best to persuade the flock of forty or so that life was worth living. The death wish is not uncommon amongst farm animals. I was once told that turkeys have so little sense that they could easily die on their feet through cold, not having the wit to find any shelter. With sheep, it seems to be a talent always to take the difficult course in life. Present them with an open gate, and they will try to charge the fence that runs next to it. Head them towards a bridge over a ditch, and they will be down the bank as if the easy way across presented some threat. Show them a bowl of feed and they will stand in it and look around them trying to guess where the smell of food is coming from. Only the collie dog has ever really mastered sheep, and if you have a dog that is not totally under your command, then you are lost.

But we were not. The flock was safely gathered in; the ewes were in one shed and the two grand sires, the Suffolk rams, were tethered to the iron gateposts, standing proud like chiefs amongst their tribe, eyeing the ewes carefully in anticipation of the mating season. We were awaiting the arrival of the man who would determine which lucky ewes were to be served by the first ram, and which would go with the other.

A car drew up, driven by a girl. Beside her was an old man, but a very lively one. There was a sparkle in his eye, a gloss on his white hair, a straightness in his back and, despite an obvious tenderness in his feet, he was out of the car and into the yard before any of us could lend a hand. He was ninety-three.

George Murray Anderson, a Scotsman born and bred but a Suffolk man by adoption, knows about sheep. He knows about Suffolk horses too. He has bred both, and risen in his time to great heights within the competitive worlds of Suffolk sheep and horses. He breaks into Burns at the slightest opportunity, and still finds time to marvel at the wonders of nature.

'Ah,' he took a deep, deep breath, '. . . that is a truly magnificent ram, truly magnificent.' His lips moistened with relish at the sight of the two chaps tethered to the gate. George, wearing a grey suit that would look well on any city gent, a grey woollen cardigan, flat tweed cap and black shiny shoes, moved over to the shed with the ewes. The yard was a foot deep in horse muck, but he trod carefully through it as one would with nearly a century's experience of doing so. I noticed later that he left the yard with shoes as clean and shiny as when he went in.

'Ah . . .' he breathed in again, 'there's some fine ewes in there, fine, fine ewes.'

'Is that right?' said Roger, swelling a little with pride.

'Magnificent!' he replied.

Then he looked carefully at the two rams. He prodded their backs, felt their hind-quarters, squeezed the back legs.

'Remember,' he said, 'we are breeding them for the butcher, and the butchers want to see some meat.'

He straightened himself up, paused, and said, 'Magnificent!'

It was decided to call one of the rams Adams for some reason, and the other was called The Other.

Each of the ewes had been given a number which had been stamped on to their backs so that when lambs were born their pedigree would be known. The numbers were taken from the ears of the sheep, which are clipped more or less at birth with a small pair of pliers. This cuts a V-shaped notch in the lamb's ear, and notches in various positions stand for different numbers and letters. It means that the parentage of every Suffolk lamb can be deduced, even several generations back. This is what the breeding business is all about. It was why George Anderson had come to Weylands Farm, since the man with the best lambs not only gets the glory but can ask the best price, and the man with the best rams sells them for a huge premium. It takes the eye of an expert to match ram and ewe to produce profitable offspring, and George's 93-year-old eye was darting from flock to rams and back again.

'Now, I should say . . .' he paused. 'Now, let me see. . . .' Roger picked up his crook ready to catch the ewe as soon as George had made his first decision. 'Let's have that lassie there, with him,' and he pointed at Adams.

In went the crook, and missed the ewe. Into the shed we all piled and cornered her, checked the number, wrote it down and shunted her into a box where she would shortly be joined by others who were to be favoured by the randy company of Mr Adams.

'I should say,' said George, becoming more Scots the harder he thought, 'that because The Other is a bit broader across the back, I'll put him with a ewe that's a bit narrower. And then,' he fixed me with his watery but precise eyes, 'we might get a lamb that's just right.' His voice rose an octave like a schoolteacher making a point. 'This,' he went on, 'is how I bred all my sheep and horses. I take the weak points and try to correct them by putting them with the right mate.'

After an hour, the ewes were in two separate sheds; the rams were still tied to the gates but their mates for the coming weeks had been decided. George sat down carefully on the edge of an old bath that was used as a manger to feed cattle. He broke into Burns: ' "Implore his counsel and assisting might, They never sought in vain that sought the Lord aright." ' And then he said nothing. We didn't break the silence. George's watery eyes looked out across the valley. It was a fine, but cool, summer's day. Corn rustled in the fields, cattle munched softly at the grass, and for once the unruly geese were content just to sit and not hiss at every passer-by.

'You'll have some magnificent lambs, Roger, that I assure you. Magnificent!'

And he took out his diary, noted the date and then looked forward to January, writing down when the first might be born. He took a cup of tea, a piece of cake, refused a 'dram', and was soon heading for the car, shoes still unsmudged by muck.

'We say that's a good sign,' said Roger, watching him go. 'We were worried last year that he might not last another twelve-month, but we always reckon that if he writes down when he thinks the lambs will be due, we say he'll stick around to see 'em.'

At that point, the huge might of Cheryl's lorry thundered into the yard. Weary after a 500-mile drive from Aberdeen, she fell out of the cab of the lorry and greeted George.

'I've got a couple of good hosses in here, George,' she announced. 'I bought 'em off the Aberdeen Council. They're going into Clydesdales! Giving up Suffolks!' She unscrewed the ramp of the lorry and lowered it with a thud. The huge rear ends of two Suffolk Punches came into view. They swayed, impatiently, as anxious to be out of that lorry as Cheryl was to be out of the cab.

They had been work-horses in the true sense, having pulled dust-carts through the streets of that granite city. George Anderson smiled as Cheryl spoke of northern parts, and inhaled the breath of Scottish air that these two animals had brought 500 miles south with them.

The first thundered down the ramp and frisked a little at the freedom and the fresh air. Roger eyed him carefully, declaring him a 'good hoss'.

Then the next. George's face lit up. 'Ah . . .' he drew breath. 'That's a fine horse. Magnificent, I would say. Magnificent.'

And he was a quite magnificent horse. He stood tall and broad. He had a flash of white hair in his brown mane and a splash of white on his back where his cart saddle would go. He was called Punch.

# Sixteen

GRUDGINGLY, the summer eventually gave us a fine day. Reasonably fine, anyway. Clouds threatened, but the air was mild and the breeze gentle, so of all the poor days to try and harvest the rye, Roger judged this to be the most promising – or the least bad. There was worry about the 1987 harvest, not only at Weylands but throughout East Anglia. Even the impregnable barley barons with their battalions of machinery were deflected from their profits by storms and rain which drenched the

corn, destroying its value as wheat to make into bread flour.

While agronomists pored over digital moisture meters on the wheat prairies of the east, while the combine-harvester drivers checked again the computer programs that now drive some of these monsters, Gerry got a rusty old file out of the forge and started to sharpen the knife of the binder.

But God, how slowly he did it. Each rasp of the file was made as slowly as if he had been polishing some fragile jewel, instead of this coarse, rusty old knife that had probably been cutting harvests since the Second World War. The clouds gathered and I feared another downpour. Feared, because as a one-day-a-week-farm-worker with only a small field of rye to cut, I might well miss harvest altogether. A horse-drawn farming year without a horse-drawn harvest! One might as well turn back from Everest with only a hundred feet to go, or walk from John o'Groat's to Penzance. Mentally I urged Gerry on, and Roger too. He was hammering away at a horse-shoe in the forge.

'That's got to be put together in the right order,' he shouted from the forge. He was bellowing at Gerry, who was about to take a hefty spanner to a seized-up wheel of the binder. Roger strode over. He unbolted a wheel here, wound another up and turned a handle, which brought a fleeting burst of life into the machine. Satisfied, he then hitched it to three horses and directed us up the hill to the field of rye.

Even though we were mobile, it was still no clearer how the binder worked, or even in which direction it would go, for in its present configuration the horses were in line with the knife but in front of it, so that any forward

129

motion of the machine was not going to do any cutting; the knife would simply slither through the corn. I hoped things would become clearer.

Roger joined us on the field.

'I got this machine off an old boy not far away,' said Roger, 'and do you know, it was all greased up and ready to go!' To discover a working binder in a greased and oiled condition was a find indeed.

With one mighty wrench of a rusty spanner and a heave at two of the wheels, the binder revealed itself in its true colours. The bushel under which it had been hiding its light was lifted when I realised that the two wheels at the back were there solely to transport the thing along the road. With those removed and the horses swung through ninety degrees, the whole apparatus became recognisable as the subject of countless harvest paintings of the first thirty years of the century, with the horses striding out in front, the driver perched atop, and the wooden sails crashing down on to the upright corn, scooping it into the cutter. After due processing, it should emerge in sheaves or tight bundles, ready to stand and dry in the blazing hot sun.

The sun was not too hot – cool, you might say, for an August day. Roger spoke softly to his horses. 'Ease up . . . ease up a bit. . . .' 'G'up' would have done for anything lighter, but Roger wanted them to feel the strain in their collars before they put their full weight into it.

The binder clattered into life.

'Swish!' and the sails came down on to the rye, slashing it and driving it into the frenzied teeth of the cutter. Pushed into the binder by the next sail, it was dragged along a canvas sheet, and then through ninety degrees and upwards. More and more of it was squeezed together when it reached the summit of its climb, until a spring gave, at which point, by some process which a million words could not describe, a greasy device threw a length of twine round the bundle, cut it just above the knot and spat it out on to the ground. True magic. (I later read that the knotter had been invented by a Canadian who was so perplexed by what he had created that his lack of understanding of it forced him to commit suicide.) Behind us was a row of sheaves, tied and tossed aside, and an avenue of spiky stubble.

We had not spat out more than a dozen sheaves when we ground to a cursing halt. So dense and thick were the stalks of rye, and so close were we to the hedges, that the binder could not scoop it up quickly enough at one end, nor eject the sheaves quickly enough from the other. Then the mysterious knotter failed on one or two occasions and we were left with untied sheaves, which meant tedious tying-up work for someone later.

'Wooah!' There was impatience in that command. Roger leapt down from the binder.

'I would normally try and do this the night before. The first two rounds are always hard work – bloody hard work.'

He grabbed handfuls of cut rye off the canvas cloths and threw them to one side, told his horses to go on and got a further ten yards before he had to jump down again. Slow work, and still a huge perimeter of field waiting to be cut before the job would get any easier.

'They often used to send an old boy round with a scythe to cut the headland before the binder arrived,' said Roger, looking disconsolately at his jammed machine again. 'And a bloody good idea it was too.' He dragged more handfuls of rye out of the machine and cut another ten yards.

He was sweating now, and reddening with a rage.

'This is the bit they don't see, this is the hard work. It all looks very nice when it's working, but it's getting it all going. I often say that these old machines are like people – they takes a bit of getting to know.'

Rupert, Courtier and Prince stood motionless, knowing better than to add to the confusion.

As the machine eventually settled into its work the pace quickened, and as the rye thinned out in places we were never halted. It was my job to walk alongside and unjam as might be required, and keep an eye out to see that the sheaves were being knotted and not thrown loose on to the field.

Cheryl was in buoyant mood that morning. 'This is real work. This'll make you sweat, lad,' and she grabbed heavy sheaves in her arms and waltzed with them like a girl with a new lover. There was total delight across her face, and indeed who could fail to be infected by this scene – golden sheaves, horses pulling hard, men at work bringing the harvest home? The air was fresh and clear and the tower of Stoke-by-Nayland church seemed as close as if it were in the next field, not three miles away. A good day for work, I thought to myself.

Roger did not do much smiling until he had completed two rounds of the field. This left a wide roadway on to which the binder could eject its sheaves, and the whole operation settled down. There would be an occasional halt to put the twine back on the knotter, or move the levers that set the point at which the knot should come, or some such minor but vital adjustment. But otherwise, the horses marched on and the machine clattered behind.

To complete this Constable landscape which we were creating for ourselves, the sheaves of rye had to be stood

132

on end to form golden pyramids which are called either 'shocks' or 'stooks', and the operation of standing them up is either 'shocking' or 'stooking', depending on which particular pub you happen to be in when the debate begins. It is one of those arguments that countrymen have amongst themselves, and where opinion can become firmly entrenched. There is even debate about the way they should stand, let alone what they are called when they are upright. Should they be stood with the knot in the twine pointing inwards, or with the knot facing outwards? There are valid reasons for doing it either way, and many a pint of foaming ale has been swilled while the point is debated.

The point of the whole business is to dry and ripen the

corn after it has been cut, so sheaves are stood on their ends a dozen at a time in such a way that the breeze can blow easily through them and dry them to a fine crispness ready to be carted away.

'You get hold of one,' said Roger, flinging his arm round a shoof like a young lad grasping a girl at a barn dance, 'then you grab another. Bang 'em 'ard on the ground and push their old heads together.' For Roger, they stood upright till two more could be hastily grabbed and stood beside them to keep the whole structure stable. When I tried, they just fell. Like threading a needle or chopping a block of wood, it is a knack. If you do not get it at the first attempt, you will certainly not get it on the second. You'll manage it on the third if you are very lucky. Or the fourth.

When two were upright you added to them till you had built yourself a cathedral of them. You could bend down and look along the whole length of the dozen pairs and peer up at the vaulted straw roof you had created. Then you grabbed two new ones and started again. And quickly too, for an extremely jovial and sharp-tongued Cheryl would not be far behind you.

Then I made a serious mistake; I rolled up my sleeves. Even though it was cool for a summer's day, half an hour of humping these sheaves to the vertical brought on a sweat, and button by button cuffs and collars were loosened. The price you pay for cooling air is stinging grazes along every exposed piece of flesh where the cut ends of the stalks rub. Sometimes they bleed a bit, but mostly they itch. They itch the length of your arms and itch in your hair where bits get lodged. Wisps of straw find their way down your shirt till your whole body is a sweaty mass of itch and your fingers are so entangled in the sheaves that to try and scratch anywhere is merely to spread more straw round your body. I thought of those jovial rural postcards of fellows in high-necked smocks heaving sheaves around fields; I had often wondered why they had never stripped sensibly to the waist, like builders. Now I know. They preferred protection to exposure and had sweated away in strawless and itchless comfort.

The binder clattered on all day. It could be heard even when out of sight, and so efficient had become its operation that when the sound of it stopped, this was a surprise rather than a matter of course. Quite a crowd gathered to see us at work. Children were brought by their grandfathers. A farmer with a thousand or more mechanised acres, but presumably a deep sentimental streak within him, dropped in and 'shocked' for an hour or so. And we worked our way round the field till all the rye was standing in stooks. Even the sheaves that fell apart where the binder had failed us and spewed out untied bundles were gathered; a length of rope was made out of twisted straw and the shoof held together with that. At four o'clock Roger unhitched the horses and walked them home. Jim Young arrived – the old tradesman, farmer and master ploughman.

'Of course,' he said, smacking his lips, 'you cut it the wrong way. You *should* have gone round the other way, you know.'

Only the satisfaction of a good day's work spared him from an extremely black look.

# Seventeen

THE summer had no sympathy, the seasons showed no remorse. No sooner had the entire field been converted by man- and horse-power from standing corn to standing sheaves than the rains poured as if compensating for a six-month drought. Thunder clapped around the farm. Not many years ago, a random fork of lightning had robbed the Clarks of the best horse they had ever owned and were ever likely to own. Was it now going to rob them of their harvest too? The mechanised farms fared no better. They could not get their combine-harvesters on to the sodden land either.

In the midst of one of many downpours, under heavy black skies that spat hail and piercing rain, the old black and white cow had a fine black calf. We weren't there when she dropped it, but she didn't need any help. It was not entirely unexpected because Roger had noticed earlier that morning that she looked ready to calve, but it wasn't until we saw the little black mite staggering around the meadow that we realised she'd performed the trick. You would never have guessed it to see the two of them: the old cow was as composed as if nothing had happened but a brief interruption to her grass-munching. And the little black calf was already on his feet and searching out the fenced limits of his new world.

The situation did, however, call for action, for the old

cow had been acting as foster mother to another calf which was now some months old and quite a hefty beast. Jealousy would prevent the older calf letting the youngster anywhere near its mother's udder, and so it was time to take the eldest calf from his foster parent and fling him on the mercy of the world.

We loaded him into the trailer and Cheryl and I drove him down the lane. The skies opened and rain poured down. The windscreen-wipers flicked across but didn't deflect any of the cascading water. We slithered off the main road down a muddy track that became softer and more rutted as we weaved our way down lanes I had never seen before. Then we went through a locked iron gate to a secret world. Nature could not have provided a more intimidating or impressive backdrop for my first glimpse of that special place.

It was a water-meadow of some forty or more acres where the Clarks kept horses that were waiting to be broken, cows waiting for the bull, horses on the mend after accidents. For the most part it seemed to be their nursery wing, where young horses could graze till they were old enough to learn the tricks of harness-work.

The air split to a mighty crack of thunder. The flash of lightning had come seconds before, so the storm centre was not far away. The rain was so heavy that it blanketed the far horizon, and only the sounds of a raging river cut through. Another crack and then, out of the gloom, like an apparition, came a galloping herd of wild horses. Manes flew, heads tossed, feet were lifted high to get them through the mud. And still they galloped up to us. I backed off but Cheryl stood her ground.

As they got closer I could see that most were Suffolks, still young and uninhibited by the experience of pulling

137

and hauling. I watched; nothing could have averted my eyes. It was like a slow-motion film – they took a long time to reach us. Then I saw there were young Shire horses too. I have seen pictures of horses roaming the Hungarian plains or the French Camargue, but never would I have believed that such a sight could have been seen in Suffolk. As they slowed, the water did not splash so high, and they slithered to a halt within feet of us – twenty or more horses whose hot breath steamed in the chilly damp air. I held out a hand, and they sniffed. Tense, they twitched and retreated when I tried to touch, but there seemed no harm in them. Then my imagination took over. I saw myself facing twenty tons of wild, unbroken and frenzied horses and backed away again. They sensed my moment of fear and a ripple of uncertainty ran through them.

Another crack, almost at the same time as the lightning, and they turned and fled, galloping back across the meadow and flinging water aside as they went.

I looked round for Cheryl. She had the calf out of the trailer and was pointing him in the direction of a couple of cows she knew were in the meadow but could not see in the darkness. She looked worried about the little calf, on his own for the first time.

'I'm sure he'll find some company. I'm sure he will,' she said to herself over and over again, and carefully locked the gate behind her.

The rain eased a little and we could see the horses, standing now by the river and all turned in our direction, watching for our next move. Her eyes wandered over each one in turn. Then she said, 'That's our future out there.' She dropped her voice, 'Our future.' After a pause, 'I hope that little calf's all right. I'll drop down tonight and just check he's all right.'

138

I never ceased to be surprised by the many faces that Cheryl Clark could present. In the mornings, before breakfast, the quick lash of her tongue was to be watched for and avoided. I remember cowering, somewhat fearful, in the corner of a dark stable while in the adjoining box a young girl who was new to the farm was being harshly criticised for the error of her mucking-out ways. Mucking out a big stable is no random task, as I overheard Cheryl Clark forcefully telling this girl. There are two principal errors: one is not getting enough mucky straw out, and the other is throwing too much clean straw away. Mrs Clark has a way she likes it done, so I noted every word carefully and turned the straw over very quietly so that she might not guess I was working next door. That way I might avoid an inspection of my work.

'I hope you're hearing this, Mr Heiney!' she called. It would be a foolish person who tried to pull the wool over her eyes.

It would also be a foolish horse who thought he might get the better of her simply because of his size compared with hers.

Take Captain, for example. Captain was a Percheron gelding. Percherons, like Suffolks, are working horses but tend to stand higher. This particular one stood higher even than most other Percherons. He was dappled with a white mane and huge crested neck; he was the best Percheron horse that Cheryl had seen in many a year. But he was four years old, and that was his trouble. Heavy horses must start to be broken to harness at two, because by the time they are much older they have worked out that they have the strength to disobey. Captain had not had the benefit of primary schooling, so his terrified owners passed him on to Cheryl to spend a term at her

139

firm, but fair, remedial college for wayward horses.

With Captain wearing a collar, bridle and a pair of ropes which were to be the reins, Cheryl set off on one of her typical horse-breaking walks around the farm. Each would be two or three miles long, and she might take four or five horses round the circuit in the course of a day, every day of the week.

Captain was nervous, to the point where the scuffling of feet behind him would have him prancing and galloping off. As he put his head down to charge away, Cheryl leant back on the ropes, but it was like trying to stop a runaway bull by putting your hand up – no amount of pressure on this horse's mouth was going to stop him.

'If he wants to go, there's nothing I shall ever be able to do to stop him.' The only aid she could call on was a length of rope tied at one end along the rein, and at the other to the hames on the collar. If she was lucky, enough pulling on this rein alone would force the horse to swing round towards her and that might stop his headlong charge. We walked on a little further, and then we brought into play the old petrol can which Cheryl had mysteriously asked me to bring. She told me to scrape it gently along the ground. One slight scrape of metal along the path, and the horse went tight and tense as if hit by a bullet. He bent his neck, wound himself into a fearful rage, and went from a walk into an attempted gallop in the distance it took for him to take one stride. I dropped the can, Cheryl hung on to the one rein that might force him to swing towards her and was dragged behind him, just managing to keep her feet. Then the mighty Captain swung towards her and stopped. We set off again.

'I've never had one like this. I'm not getting anywhere . . .' she said, over and over again.

We reached the top of the hill and came alongside a pile of sugar beet that a neighbouring farmer had recently lifted.

'I remember,' said Cheryl, 'coming up here with a pair of young Shire horses that were working side by side in harness for the first time. There was a guy in a tractor standing with a bucket on the front end, and he was scooping up beet. Just as we went past, he dropped the load into an iron tank. You've never heard such a noise. Well, those two horses, they took off. I stood up and put all my weight on the reins, but I couldn't stop 'em. One of 'em started kicking out at the wood I was standing on. Well, I couldn't help it. I fell forward and grabbed hold of the pole (between the two frightened galloping horses) and I tried my best to hang on. Them buggers, they just galloped. I thought, This is it, this is the end!

'Well, I hung on as long as I could and managed to fall on the ground clear of the horses' feet, thank God. But I was towing an old tractor tyre behind the cart to give it a bit more drag. Well, that old tyre, that went right over me and I just lay in the road. Well, a car came round the corner and nearly ran me over. The chap got out; he said, "Are you all right?" I said, "I don't know if I'm all right or not, mate." Meanwhile, the horses had found their way home, would you believe. Found their way home! Well, I went to hospital. I was covered in blood but they couldn't find anything broken. So when I got home, Roger said, "You'll get stiff, you know, if you don't work." So that's what I did. I went to plough. I ploughed half an acre that afternoon!'

'Walk on, Captain,' she muttered to the horse, who was settling a little. 'There's a good boy. Look, he's better now. We'll get there in the end with him, we'll get there.'

There is a lot to be learnt from working alongside horse-men, but not half as much as can be discovered by being in sole charge of a cart-horse, and with a job of work to do. I had now been nearly eight months on the farm, and so it was expected that I could be trusted with a horse without having to keep running back for instructions or setting off on jobs without vital bits of harness, or forget-ting something as silly as a fork.

A morning in late September dawned cool, but bright and clear – the clarity that comes to East Anglia only when the wind swings into the wilder and chillier north-west. The sunshine was welcome and uplifting, warming too if you managed to find a job that kept you out of the breeze. It made the usually steamy early-morning work of feeding, grooming and watering that much more accept-able, but the price to be paid was that it was now becom-ing noticeable that the sun was rising later every day.

My orders for the day were to take a horse and tumbril and fetch a load of hay from a farm a few miles away; 'Mrs Wear's place', Roger called it. On such a glorious day, with the freshness in the air and the sweet smell of the hay to look forward to, there could be no finer job. The horse was to be Punch, one of the Suffolks that Cheryl had brought back from Scotland a month or so ago and who was now getting back into the way of working for his living. He lived in a box at the back of the yard alongside his old mate from Scotland, who was called Star. They made a good pair, everyone said so. They weren't a perfect match as far as colour and shape were concerned, but in terms of temperament and ability to work together, they were reckoned to be first-class. 'That'll be a shame to split up a pair like that when we sell 'em. Right shame, that'll be,' said Cheryl.

I brushed Punch and got him ready for the road. I was learning the knack of heaving the great collar on to his head: upside down to get it over the breadth of his head, and twisting it till it fell back on his broad chestnut shoulders. Horse collars for Suffolk Punches can be massive affairs, made heavy by the sheer volume of leather and bulky by virtue of the tightly packed straw with which they are stuffed. Around them fit the wooden hames, usually painted red with black tips. It is to these that the chains are attached which will connect to whatever the horse is pulling, be it plough or cart. It all adds up to a fair old weight, and if the horse is in any way reluctant to take his collar and flings his head in the air it is even more of a load to be carrying on upstretched arms.

But Punch took his collar, and even generously dipped his head to help. Then I quickly threw the cart saddle on to his back. The cart saddle has a wooden groove across it into which the back-chain on the cart falls to carry the weight of the shafts. The cart saddle also connects to the 'breechings', an assortment of leather straps that help the horse to push the cart backwards if needs be. Fairly sure that I had it all in the right order, I slipped on the bridle.

I have always been deeply impressed by the ability of these Suffolk horses to wriggle themselves out of the tightest corners even with their rear vision restricted by blinkers. 'Get back, old hoss,' I muttered to Punch and he started to reverse out of his stall. His rump collided with the doorpost and so he edged forward and tried again, shuffling this way and that till he found the gap he was looking for. Then he managed to back into a pointed harness-hook that would have had a lighter horse leaping through the roof, but he just edged forward an inch or two, and when he decided he had gone far enough he backed again and made sure he missed it next time.

We were soon in the yard and walking slowly up to the tumbril, which had its shafts pointing high in the air. I turned Punch, backed him slowly and swung his head this way and that until he was beneath the shafts and between them, then I lowered them till the chain fell across the groove in the saddle and then carried out the rest of the connections with chains on both sides. Punch was successfully harnessed. It was a good start.

Needless to say, something had been forgotten. It was the plough line: a length of stout cord that could be used as reins. Roger knotted an end to each side of the bit and led them to the back of the tumbril as a sort of emergency rope to grab if for any reason the horse decided to make a run for it. I hopped, or tried to hop, into the tumbril, but it was far too high and what should have been the athletic leap of an agricultural worker turned into a groaning and heaving scrabble while I tried to get my leg high enough in the air to make the back of the cart. All the time I was talking to the horse: 'Good lad . . . stand still . . . good boy . . . Whoa,' and all the time the horse was twitching and ready to go.

Successfully mounted, I took hold of the reins and told him to 'G'urrp'. He leaned into his collar, slowly took up the weight and with slow, measured and heavy footsteps he ambled up the lane and towards the road. We were going fine until we came to a right turn which led to the meadow – not the direction in which I wished to go. We got into what Roger would have called a 'muddle'. The horse wanted to head for the meadow and tasty green grass, and I wanted him to carry on along the dull and unappetising tarmac road. So he bent his head to the right and I pulled the plough line to try and stop him.

144

Keeping hold of the plough line, I jumped down from the tumbril rather faster than I had got up and cried, 'You old sodding horse. . . .' It did the trick; he turned his head towards the road and, realising that his escape plan had been thwarted, he plodded on in the right direction. Not wishing to have another argument at the next inviting lane that he thought might lead to a tasty meadow, I decided to lead him by walking alongside him. He didn't put another foot wrong.

Once the horse had settled and got over his initial excitement at having been sent on a job of work, Punch settled into a contented and measured stride. He bellowed occasionally, and made piercing whinnying noises; but this was only a call to his old friend Star whom he had left behind in the stable. The horsy chat echoed around the fields, and in the far distance Star's plaintive and lonely reply could be heard cutting through the air.

We turned right at the village, did another couple of hundred yards on the main road and then bore left down a narrowing lane till we turned on to a track. Like so many turns off the beaten track in this part of Suffolk, the effort was well rewarded, for the path narrowed until it became no more than a cart-track which meandered through elderly woodland. No modern plantation of dreary evergreens, but a wealth of beech, oak and ash with leaves beginning to show their ruddy autumn colours in the penetrating light of the sun. There was a little more of a chill now, and Punch's breath turned to steam the moment it was out of his nostrils. I felt the warmth of him as I held the lead rein, and was pleased to feel it too, for the new sharpness of the breeze sent a shiver through me.

We came to our first gate. Clearly, to get through meant

letting go of the horse not only when I went to open it, but also when I closed it behind us. Would he stand, would he charge off? I thought it was unlikely that he would bolt, but how could I be sure? I stopped him just a couple of feet away from the gate, checking which way it opened. I told him firmly and sharply to '*Stand still!*' He froze. I sprinted to the gate, flung it open and quickly grabbed the leading rein to walk him through. That was the easy part, for I was always ahead of the horse and could stop him by grabbing the rein if necessary.

Shutting the gate again was not quite so simple; it meant letting the horse stand while I went behind him. I thought of the plough line that Roger had rigged for me. I checked how it ran round the back of the tumbril in case I needed it in a hurry. I told him to '*Stand still!*' again, judged him to be settled and then ran and slammed the gate shut. Needless to say, the horse did not move an inch. He had been through more gates in his short lifetime than I had in mine. I was beginning to understand that horsemanship was as much about learning from the horse as it was about teaching the horse what was required, and from that moment on I was happy to let Punch teach me all that he knew – which was clearly quite a lot.

I don't quite know how I feel about bullocks. Are they playful young things, mere children who only seek out of life fun and food, and have not yet attained an age where malice might cross their minds? By God, I hoped so, for as we came through the gate and turned along the winding path that stretched for at least half a mile through the meadow, I saw a herd of about a hundred bullocks – coming our way. What would Punch do? Might he run a mile, and what would I do to catch him? Was I being

146

foolish in taking him through the meadow in the first place and what mirth might it give to Roger and Cheryl if I returned home in cowardly fashion and without the load, saying that the bullocks turned us back? Like a very slow re-run of the Charge of the Light Brigade, Punch and I marched on with our heads high into the jaws of death, pretending to be oblivious of the slowly advancing herd.

Slowly they came, and then the first of the bullocks broke into a trot, followed by the rest. They formed up in a battle line, but instead of confronting us, took interest only in the tumbril and what fodder it might contain. Punch plodded on. Only when a wet, anxious and over-inquisitive bovine nose came too close did Punch fling his head up with a start; but I calmed him, and told him to walk on and ignore the children behind.

The gate at the far end of the meadow did not arrive too soon. Sweating with exertion and a certain amount of fear, I told Punch to '*Stand*', took up a stick and flailed it around till the bullocks backed off just far enough for me to get the gate open and the horse through. Punch stood perfectly still once again while I slammed the gate and breathed a huge sigh.

Passing through the gate, I saw that we were now in the yard of what, in its day, must have been a huge and thriving farm. Its great wooden barns must have housed tons of grain, the fenced yards would have been for cattle, and within the tarred, wooden complex would have been a stable full of working Suffolk horses, perhaps as many as a dozen. But it was silent now, except for the rumble of the tumbril as we made our way towards the pile of hay, and the rattle of the gate behind us where the bullocks were still nudging the chain with their noses. We turned

147

past an old cart-shed, empty of carts, and came to a smaller, inner yard outside the huge barn. I backed Punch up to the heap of hay, and to ensure that he didn't wander off I just put a log in front of the wheel of the tumbril, and told him to '*Stand still*'. He stood, mostly still. He edged backwards and forwards a little and every ten minutes or so I had to move the log, but he made a good companion as I worked in the yard of this silent old farm. We were like a pair of ghosts.

I chatted a bit, broke off from forking the hay to give him a mouthful of it, which he seemed to appreciate, and generally enjoyed this magical little corner of Suffolk, shrouded as it was in complete silence, except for Punch's munching and his shuffling feet.

Roger had told me to expect to bump into Mrs Wear, who lived in the farmhouse, so her appearance was no surprise. A tiny lady, with a face as grained and weathered as the wooden boarding of the old barn, she had wrapped herself tightly in an old raincoat.

'Not a bad day,' she said.

'No, not a bad day at all,' I replied, lifting my voice and assuming that she was deaf. 'I've come for a bit of hay,' I offered.

'Y'p, you've come for a bit a hay,' and her voice tailed off. I swept another forkful on to the tumbril and turned towards her, desperately wondering where I might take the conversation next, but she had vanished.

The hay was now piled high on the tumbril in a magnificent heap. Judging it to be enough, I threw a rope over the top to keep it in place and tied it securely.

'Tie that down or that'll blow,' came a faltering voice from behind. It was Mrs Wear again, who had materialised with the speed at which she had just vanished. I assured

148

her that I'd make certain it was secure, tied a few more knots while she was watching to let her know that I had got the message, and saw her make her way across the yard to the big black barn. Just as I heard the heavy door of the barn shut behind her, I suddenly remembered the bullocks, and thought of asking her to hold the gate open for me and then close it again, which would be the most difficult part of this operation since the return journey gave the bullocks ample time to make a break for it and be through the gate into the yard. I felt that I could do without complications like that.

I told Punch to stand still (although he had hardly moved an inch) and I ran after Mrs Wear towards the barn. I opened the door and peered into the gloom, startling a bird or two with the creak of the door. The dim, dusty shafts of light that came through gaps in the tiles and sliced through the darkness gave enough light for me to see up to the high roof. It was supported on a web of naturally curving oak beams joined with mighty pegs, no nails or bolts. It was like a church, complete with wooden vaulted roof and a stillness of sanctity about. It even had a nave and huge doors either end of the transepts, which would have been opened on threshing days to allow the wind to blow away the chaff from the corn.

I looked all over the place, but could see no Mrs Wear. I called out, but the only reply was my echoing voice. I looked around but I could see no other way out, no way she could have escaped from the barn without coming through the door in which I was standing; but she was not there. I was certain that I saw her go in, but never saw her come out. I shuddered a little as a breeze swept over me, and went back to Punch, who was standing with his load and hadn't moved an inch.

149

Luckily, a tractor driver turned up and held the gate for us, and, taking all our courage in our hands, Punch and I made for the battleground of the great meadow, where the battalion of bullocks were waiting for our return. We swept them aside like a frigate ploughing through the ocean. Some of them took the opportunity to steal a mouthful of hay, but we must have already delivered most of our entertainment value and gradually the party broke up, the bullocks dispersing to do whatever bullocks do all day. By the time we were halfway across the meadow they had left us in peace, and Punch and I made our way merrily towards the gate.

The homeward journey saw thoughts flashing across my mind, thoughts of what a waste it would be to allow this newly found enthusiasm of mine for the working horse to be extinguished when the year came to its end. Enthusiasm is perhaps not strong enough a word; obsession might just do it justice. I had bought every book of nineteenth-century agriculture that I could either find or afford. My bible had become *Stephen's Book of the Farm*, written by a dogmatic old Scot in 1866. It had detailed instructions on dry-stone-walling, a chapter on the 'Value of Straw' and the 'Evils of Impure Air' in animal housing. I could give you chapter and verse on everything from extracting a dead calf to preparing turnips for sheep. Of course, I had much that was quite up to date; some of it had even been written this century. *The Science and Practice of British Farming* by Watson and Moore was a particular favourite, although it had a modernist veneer, having been written as recently as 1933. Even as late as the 1930s, it was assumed that ploughing and carting would be done entirely by horse, although the chugging of the tractor must have been creeping ever closer.

The joke is that these books, sold now as curiosity pieces, contain much that is relevant to the running of Weylands Farm. They are all books that Roger keeps as sources of information, haphazardly stuffed on the shelves of the farm office, which also sports an aged typewriter and a roll-top desk behind which a gentleman farmer might have sat with dignity, 'tut-tutting' over the bill from the corn chandler. No modern manual on 'Pneumatic Fertiliser Injection' had any place at Weylands, or in my heart for that matter. Any book that told you how to give a horse a good laxative 'physic' was of far more appeal than a million words on combine harvesters.

So, out of loyalty to the Clarks' principles and out of genuine interest, I devoured the old books with the passion of a teenage girl who has just discovered Mills and Boon. I read them on trains and during breaks at motorway service areas, and got funny looks from my fellow passengers as I turned over page after page of illustrations on the principles of muck-heap building, ditch-digging, pig-farrowing and dung-spreading. I kept these books by my bedside too, and would offer my wife an occasional earful on the problems of sheep scab.

I suppose what it boiled down to, and what I eventually decided on that trudge back to the farm with Punch and the load of hay, was that the working of the land in a traditional way was now a part of my life which I would not be able to shed. I was lucky in that I had a home in the country and had just acquired five acres of land on which to play at farming, so why should I not try it for myself, part-time at least? Why not see if I could put just a fraction of the effort into it that the Clarks do, and reap a fraction of the rich satisfaction on which they thrive? Plans started to form in my mind. If I bought Punch, I thought, I could get some harness and an old tumbril, and perhaps grow some mangels for him to eat in the winter . . . or some maize which he likes to chew . . . or perhaps make hay, and cart it as I was now doing. These were the dreams that formed on that slow walk through the meadow and woods, as I glanced first at Punch and then at the fields and finally at the castles I was building in the air. When we got back to Weylands Farm I confronted Cheryl.

'You said Punch was up for sale. Well, if he is I'd like to buy him.'

Cheryl looked slightly astonished. 'I'd never known you'd be interested, otherwise I wouldn't have asked this other chap to come and have a look. But I'm afraid he's coming at the weekend. I'm very sorry.'

I was sorry too, very sorry. But I consoled myself with the thought that there'd be other horses passing through the yard, just as good as old Punch. I was certain that this chap, whoever he was, would buy him, for everyone who saw him said he was a fine horse and a good example of a Suffolk Punch. He would certainly not disgrace himself in the show-ring.

Never mind. I forked the hay off the tumbril, took the horse to the trough, where he sucked up a good few gallons, and led him to his stall and his feed. I gave him a good hefty pat as thanks for an intensive and, for me, important morning.

# Eighteen

I TRIED throughout the year to be as regular in my farm visits as I could. I had set out to do one day a week for a year, and if for any reason I was forced to miss a week the frustration was overwhelming. Roger mentioned that he thought there were few jobs on the farm that I had missed, but one in particular that I was sad not to have been part of was the gathering of the harvest of rye, especially having 'stooked' it sheaf by sheaf. But in a sodden year such as this had been, no farmer could wait for any one man when the weather was right and a vital job like bringing home the harvest had to be done. So the next time I wandered up the long lane to what they called the Pill Box field, huge stacks of rye stood proudly in a corner.

They had a regularity of shape that came from careful building rather than random flinging of sheaf upon sheaf. I imagined the cursing and muttering that must have been spat from Gerry's lips as he fought every wisp of straw with his pitchfork. The entertainment value apart, I would have enjoyed seeing the stacks being built and watching how the sheaves were laid and how the top was thatched to keep the grain dry till it was time to be threshed. The combine-harvester has dispensed with the talents of the men who could build a stack. Now it is a matter of chop-chop at one end, and grain spewed out at the other. There is no intermediate stage. No agricultural architecture.

However, it was always reassuring to find a job on the land that no piece of advanced machinery had ever bothered to master and for which the horse was still well suited. One such was the lifting and carting of the bulbous red mangels. These swollen and succulent roots are lifted before the first frosts catch them, and then stored under earth and straw in what is called a 'clamp' to keep the nip of the winter air off them. By some natural chemical process the roots sweeten as the winter months pass, and by the time it is Christmas mangel is fodder as sweet to cattle, sheep and horses as Christmas pudding is to us.

The problem with lifting mangels, as Roger explained to me, is in cutting off the green leafy tops without taking a slice off the root, otherwise exposure to the air will cause it to rot in the heap and the rot will spread to the other succulent beauties. That in itself is a problem that can be solved with care, but the mangel-lifting needs care *and* speed if five acres are to be lifted; and this, I saw, was only to be achieved by an impressive deftness with a knife.

Roger asked for four horses to be made ready. Two would be in the shafts of tumbrils and the other two horses would act as trace horses and help haul each loaded tumbril up the slithery muddy hill to the yard. A load of mangels must weigh over a ton, and on the slippery and steep track it wasn't certain that a horse on his own would be able to manage it. While two of the horses took a load home, we would be loading the other tumbril and so the work need never stop.

Roger appeared with a collection of extremely well

sharpened carving knives, removed from the kitchen. There were five of us working on the field and each of us was given one.

'Take your knife in one hand,' Roger demonstrated, 'and then pull your mangel out of the ground. You put your knife under it, like that, and then with a flick you fling it into the air. As you do that, the knife slices the top off, and the mangel flies into the tumbril.' And to prove that it did, he cut one with a flourish of his knife and a deftness of arm movement. With a thud, the neatly topped and unscarred mangel landed in the tumbril and the green leaf fell limply to the ground. Then I tried, I flicked, and missed; picked it up again and flicked once more, but with no visible effect on the mangel. So I developed my own beheading technique which may not have been as sporty as Roger's, but at least got the tops cut off.

I watched Roger drive the horses up the hill, dragging the massive load up the steep muddy slope. He walked alongside them, driving the trace horse on plough lines and the horse between the shafts with the leading rein, just as we had done when carting muck in the snow ten months ago. A fine sight it looked set against the backdrop of the farmyard and the hills beyond. The two horses were Punch and Star. I didn't have the courage to ask if the man had been to see Punch yet, and whether he was sold. I wondered about Star.

'I'll get a thrashing gang together for the next time you come, and we'll thrash out that wheat,' was Roger's promise, and true to his word I arrived to find half a dozen men standing beside a tarpaulin-clad, wooden monster and alongside it an unfamiliar piece of equipment for Weylands Farm: a tractor. I call it a tractor, but nobody else would flatter it by bestowing such a title on it. It had all the parts in roughly the right places but when it came to providing traction, which was its sole purpose in life, it hardly looked man enough for the job. That rounded, heavily bearded and jovial fellow Tom Walne seemed to be in charge – a sort of gang-leader who was marshalling his men to various stations. In his way, he too was part of a dying rather than expanding tradition. I suppose he would have been described as a carter: a man who moved things around the countryside for people. But there was more to him than that. He was a man who could turn a hand to any job from fencing to welding, but you couldn't call him a farm-worker. He fitted into no particular slot, like so many who passed through Weylands Farm. But he certainly understood the innards of the thrashing machine, which was no mean intellectual feat.

Layer after layer of protective canvas and tarpaulin were slid back to reveal this remarkable machine in all its faded glory. It was basically a huge wooden box standing on four wheels. It must have been ten feet high by twenty feet long, but size was difficult to judge for it was such an overpowering piece of machinery that it was all I could do to prevent myself from just standing and staring and enjoying the complexity of it, especially the array of cogs, gears, wheels and drive-belts that adorned one side of it. I had seen one before, in a museum, but never one that had its living to earn.

'My uncle had one of these,' said Roger proudly, while Tom tried to coax the tractor into life. 'His father set him up in business with one, and a steam engine to drive it, all for £100. He used to take it round the countryside from field to field, thrashing out for various farmers.'

Thrashing is the final but vital stage in converting grown corn into cash. The machine separates the grain from the stalk and the husk and spews them out in three different directions. The corn goes into sacks at one end and is sold, chaff (which is mainly the husks and called 'flight') pours from another hole and might feed stock in the winter, and out of the rear end pours straw for bedding. It is a remarkable machine, that does not allow any part of the carefully grown plant to go to waste.

The theory of its operation is simple but, as with much of the machinery from that agricultural era, the practice is more difficult to understand and almost impossible to describe. I asked Roger what went on inside and he told me of the 'drum' and how it spun round, beating the corn as it went. With half an understanding I then asked Tom how the thing worked and got a different tale, so I decided that the thrashing machine was to be one of the wonders of the world that was to be enjoyed for its beauty, and not questioned.

There was a cloud of black smoke as the tractor eventually marshalled its pistons into some semblance of the correct order in which to fire, and, satisfied that the throbbing and chugging were likely to continue, Tom leapt down and called for the canvas drive-belt which was to be the link between the midget of a tractor and the might of the thrashing drum. It was unrolled along the ground, spreading out like a carpet; one end was slipped over a wheel on the thrashing machine and the other over a small flywheel sticking out of the side of the tractor. Tom leapt up again, backed the tractor till the belt came tight and called to all around to stand clear. He gave a blast on the horn and slipped the tractor into gear, causing the flywheel to start turning – and with it the belt.

157

There was a slow rumble, not unlike the sound of distant heavy artillery fire, and the rumble grew louder, like an approaching thunderstorm, as every wheel and gear in the thrashing machine started to turn for the first time in twelve months. Not only did wheels turn, but eccentric cams on shafts made thin battens of wood rock from side to side. As the machine gathered speed it started to rock gently, backwards and forwards on its wheels at first and then from side to side. Satisfied that the monster was not going to explode with the effort of simply turning, I moved in for a closer look and saw a faded drawing pinned to the side of the machine which showed the complex but vital arrangement of what must have been a dozen drive-belts. Any belt not turning meant some part of the machine not functioning, and so Tom took himself on a tour of inspection through the whirring lacings of the machine.

Roger was busy with a roll of wire netting. I didn't like to ask why but watched as he carefully unrolled it, and with stakes built a fence round three sides of the stack of corn that was to be thrashed. Gerry appeared, armed as ever with his favourite pitchfork, and just looked. He did and said nothing.

The machine was declared in good order. It had Tom Walne's personal seal of approval and the thrashing could now commence. The 'drum', as the machine is also known, was standing beside the stack, and Roger and another man clambered to the top. On the top of the drum was a hole big enough to allow sheaves to be thrown in but hopefully prevent a man falling in, although it has been known. Another man, Norman, was in charge of that end of the operation.

Roger stuck his fork into the first sheaf and tossed it to

Norman on the drum. He picked it up with a knife which he stuck beneath the baler twine that held it together, and with an upward sweep the sheaf was cut and fell into the drum, leaving the short length of twine still in the man's hand.

As the first sheaf was flung into the hole, the machine groaned like a foodmixer that has had a handful of grit thrown into it, or an engine fighting a battle with sand in its petrol. It groaned even more as the next sheaf was thrown in, and then settled into a contented motion.

'They used to have old rhymes, you know,' said Roger. ' "Feed me well and keep me clean, And I'll drive the drum with a lot less steam." ' This, he explained, referred to the steam engine that would have done the job that Tom's rusty old tractor was doing.

'And the drum keeps saying,' Roger continued, 'more ... more ... more. . . .' I listened to the sounds coming from the thrashing machine, and indeed the rhythmical rumble did sound like a pleading for 'more ... more. . . .'

'Then the straw pitcher that picks up the straw and carries it to the top of the stack, that has a verse of its own,' said Roger. 'It goes, "Clickety, clack, clickety, clack, Keep me clear or I'll take it back." ' This meant that the man on the stack had to be sharp with his fork or the straw would be on the ground instead of on top of the growing heap.

'The secret is in feeding at the right rate,' said Roger from atop the stack. 'You've got to feed it right to get it to work at its best.' In went another sheaf. Mangle, rumble, grind, splatter – all these sounds together drowning the faltering put-put of the uncertain tractor engine.

And then, as if some magic trick had been performed before our very eyes, a slow trickle of precious grain started to appear. It fell gently at first into an old zinc tank, and when there was enough of it it was sucked upwards through a pipe and into a waiting trailer. Hard-won grains, thrashed from the sheaves, trickled at an ever-increasing rate into the hopper. The sensation of seeing it flow, the culmination of a season's ploughing, sowing and reaping, cannot be unlike seeing oil spurt from a newly drilled well or grains of gold sparkle in the bottom of a prospector's pan.

But the by-products were not being forgotten. From a hole a foot square at the side of the now gently rocking, rumbling machine poured the husks which had protected the grain through its growing life. Stuart, Roger's mate in the forge, was assigned the task of ensuring that none of this went to waste. Of course, a combine-harvester discards it with the straw, but when a long winter looms with no prospect of a blade of fresh grass to feed an animal something as belly-filling as 'flight' is to be treasured.

It poured into huge black sacks which seemed to be the size of hot-air balloons, but even when full they could be tossed around as easily as if they had been stuffed with feathers.

Expecting an answer measured in months I called to Roger, 'How long will the flight last you?' Roger was now noticeably less high in the sky as the stack dwindled.

'We get through three bags a day,' he said coolly. I walked to the far end of the machine, where Gerry was leaning on his pitchfork waiting for some action. Out of that end of the machine were slowly emerging long lengths of straw which Gerry eyed as they advanced towards him. Our time had come.

Gerry nodded in the direction of a fork that was lying on the ground, which I took to be an instruction to pick it up. Gerry then armed himself with his and took forkful after forkful of the emerging straw and laid it as if building the foundations of a square house. I tried to help by adding a forkful myself, but I was sharply told by Gerry that I was simply to pass the straw to him and he would do the building. It may seem a simple and not very skilful job to pick up a bundle of straw with a fork but Gerry had turned it into an art, and should not be mocked for it. Roger had once told me that Gerry was a 'good man with a fork', and here, on this emerging strawstack, the maestro was on top form. He didn't simply dig the fork in and take what happened to stick to it, as a child might when learning to eat peas with a knife and fork. Rather, he'd ram the fork into the straw till he had a tight bundle on the end, then ram it home again to get even more. Yes, a good man with a fork is an education to watch.

'Wooah,' shouted Tom Walne with an urgency in his voice as he ran to the tractor, sounded the horn and knocked her out of gear. In the quiet that ensued, the idle flapping of a broken belt told us that this was a good time for tea. Roger jumped down from the stack, Tom took off his cap and scratched his head, then Roger declared, 'I've got the very thing,' and slithered down the bank towards his forge, where his treasure chest of odds, ends and general spares might contain the vital part that would save the day.

In former times, of course, the stopping of the drum might have been sabotage. 'Them old boys,' Roger told me once, 'they used to have a stick with them, and when they wanted a breather, they'd just flick one of the belts off when the guvnor wasn't watching. No one was allowed to rest, you see. It was the only way they could get a break.'

We supped hot tea sitting on the big black sacks of chaff, and waited. Eventually Roger appeared clutching a leather belt from a pair of trousers. With a heave, he and Tom tightened the buckle and guessed that that would do the job. We slung the dregs of the tea on to the ground and, with a blow on the hooter and a 'put-put' from the tractor, the mighty drum was back in action. 'More, more, more,' it rumbled. 'Lousy, bloody old straw,' cursed Gerry as she spewed at us once again.

The square foundations of the strawstack having been laid, Gerry now started to fill the inside, but always in such a way that the walls were higher than the middle and the eventual stack would be stable and not inclined to topple over. A straight stack, they say, is the trademark of a well-run farm. My new responsibility was to ensure that the straw was well trodden after the master architect had placed it precisely where he wanted it. As the stack grew higher, the pile of sheaves on which Roger was standing shrank until we were level. Like two lifts passing, we were on the way up and Roger was on the way down.

Suddenly a squeal rang out. 'Yip, yip, yip . . .' cried Roger in a high-pitched voice, and all the others joined in. Down below, the first of the rats was leaving the sinking ship. Rats who had lived quite happily amongst the sheaves were now finding life a little too exposed, and as they made their hasty escape they were soon up against the wire-netting. Then the dogs went in. Two little terriers with razor teeth took on the rats face to face in what was by no means a certain contest. If a rat managed to get away, it then fell to the men to try and spike it with a pitchfork, but on the whole the terriers were more efficient.

The excitement of the kill was only a brief interruption

to the work. More and more sheaves rattled into the drum, and mounds of straw poured forth to bolster Gerry's amazing edifice. As the stack of unthrashed corn dwindled, so the mood became lighter, not only because the end of the job was in sight, but because the effort of the work had been replaced by a rhythm which halved the burden of the task. The chugging of the tractor and the rumble of the drum were our metronome, and we flung sheaves and tossed straw with the togetherness of an orchestra – until there were no more sheaves to thrash.

By four o'clock, the covers were going back on the thrashing machine, the tractor was silenced and the air began to clear of the dust that endlessly flew out of the machine as it worked its magic. Then came the time to move it to its new position, well out of the way, where it could stand till thrashing came around again, probably not till next winter. The feeble tractor was hooked on to it and the engine revved, but with little result. The tractor wheels slithered in the mud and the mighty machine didn't budge an inch. While another tractor was being sent for, Cheryl appeared.

'Get four horses on that, you'll shift it!' was her suggestion. It was the first time that day that horses had crossed my mind. High technology had taken over, for a short time anyway.

# Nineteen

I CAN'T quite remember how I came to buy Punch. I think I must have been stunned by the news that the chap who had come to see him didn't want to buy him. It wasn't Punch that was the problem, it was his old mate Star, who had some trouble with his skin which would keep him for ever out of the show-ring, though he was sound enough for farm-work. As this chap was looking for a pair of show-horses and not just one, he had to say no thanks to Punch. So he became mine.

Owning a Suffolk horse was a daunting prospect, frightening even. Not because I hadn't kept horses before, for I already had two Fell ponies at home. It was simply the thought of being in charge of something so majestic, so powerful, so totally overwhelming as a Suffolk horse that made me shiver for just a second when Cheryl broke the news that I could have him if I wanted. It is one thing to be in charge of other people's horses, where someone else will take the ultimate responsibility; it is another to have only yourself, and the horse, to answer to.

I wandered round to Punch's box to give him a bit of a pat, hoping that this would be the start of a great relationship, but as I patted he merely rolled his eye, showing the whites as horses do when in an uncertain frame of mind. I patted again, and he didn't look the slightest bit pleased. It was nearly feeding time and pats were no substitute for grub, not for a horse.

Gilchrist LRPS

*Weylands Farm, Suffolk*

*Cheryl Clark 'collaring-up'*

Shead

Annie Shead

*Suffolk Punches, ready for work*

*At plough*

Annie Shead

I. H. Gilchrist LRPS

*Ploughing my own furrow*

*Fighting the reversible plough*

Tim Fargher

*Harrowing spring corn*

*Cheryl Clark cutting corn: three Suffolks and a binder*

*Threshing day*

*Shockin' or
stookin' strings
in or out?*

*Gerry thatching the corn stack*

I. H. Gilchrist LRPS

*Carting mangels—cold October work*

*Prince, me and the Manchester Corp. dust cart, Suffolk Show 1987*

*With Roger and Gerry—while the horses take a break*

Roger Smith

*Roger Clark, the supreme showman*

I gave poor old Star a glance as I left the stable. He was a darker coloured horse, stockier in many ways and what Cheryl had called a 'good old-fashioned Suffolk Punch'. He and Punch had been together for years now, working in Scotland, carting rubbish, giving rides. I remembered how Punch had bellowed for his mate when we went on that long walk through the bullock field for hay. They'll miss each other, I thought to myself.

There was one immediate effect of my new acquisition, and that was to inject a new urgency into the early morning scanning of the local newspaper. It is called the *East Anglian Daily Times*, and although it faithfully reports the up and downs of governments at home and abroad, and more importantly the deliberations of the local fathers on the council, none of this compares in news value with the classified column headed 'Auctioneers' Announcements'. This is where the gold can be found if only you have the patience and the instinct to pan for it. You start by looking at the items for sale in the auctioneers' published lists, and if there is a variation of 'agricultural bygones' you send for a catalogue straight away. When Roger and I spotted a sale which advertised 'various cart-horse harnesses', we put it in the diary without a second thought.

We arrived at the sale ground, which was actually on the farm that was being sold up. The smaller items were displayed as carefully as in a West End shop window, and in a magnificent setting of huge thatched oak barns of great age and dignity. No shop-window dresser could have provided a better backdrop for what was to be sold.

But what exactly was to be sold? There were wooden machines that seemed to work, but what they did was anyone's guess. The catalogue did not go out of its way to shed any light. What was a 'Hall's Patent Clock Gun' or a 'sack stand and bagging strap'? And why was there a 'wicker wheelchair on three wheels'? Had mere ownership of this miscellany of curious bygones, antiques and junk reduced the poor owner to an invalid?

I thought of Punch and the plans I had made in my head for when my time at Weylands Farm was over. I wondered about doing a bit of carting with him, and thought I might bid for the tumbril. There was a root-slicer in the corner, just like Roger's; it was even stamped 'Great Unchokable' like the one that Gerry wound with as much solemnity as if he were in sole charge of turning the earth on its axis. I must have one of those, so I made a note to bid. Ploughs were a bit beyond me, but Roger was eyeing a rare Reversible. I was sad to see that the harness which looked so good in the catalogue pictures was in fact a poor lot and clearly a relic from days when cart-horses were smaller than the Suffolk Punches of today. There wasn't going to be much here for Punch, I thought.

Experience and sound knowledge are wonderful things to have at a farm sale and so Roger, having plenty of both, was able to spot amongst a heap of rotting horse collars, *the* one that was worth buying and renovating. He also spotted four tins of Black Harness Oil, which is now no longer made but which he thinks is better for harness than the preparations you can buy today. He unscrewed the tops off the rusty tins, took a sniff and declared it to be good stuff. (He bought it, and later discovered one to be concentrated sheep dip!)

The bidding started. It is always a tense moment for me, because I am sure that everyone else at the sale has only come for the things that I want to buy. Usually, that all-important sense of proportion about how much I pay is overridden by an urgent desire to own. These things can get out of hand. I didn't mind paying £11 for the harness rack, or £18 for three old cart saddles that Roger thought worth the money. But why did I pay £12 for a chopping block that was no more than a bit of tree trunk? The answer is probably because someone at the sale had just said to me, 'That's an old stable block. When those old boys got tired they used to talk about going to have "five minutes on the block".'

Well, it seemed a plausible tale and I swallowed it. When I tried to check this fable out with Roger, needless to say he'd never heard of it. I nearly fell for a 'quantity of pea tripods' and was very tempted by an air-raid siren, but with my eye still on the tumbril I held back.

When it came to Lot 247, 'a tip tumbril with shafts', quite a few people were gathered round what was really a very elderly cart with as many worms eating their way through it as there were nails holding it together. Roger thought it was worth a hundred quid, and I thought I'd pay that but no more. Within seconds the bidding was up to two hundred quid and the two bidders who were locked in combat had that look in their eye that said they would go much further than that. Clearly, sense was not going to prevail; although there were quite a few of us there who would have gone higher, there was a silly battle taking place and we knew when to withdraw. It finally fell for £500 to a man whose father had built it many years before. He deserved to get it cheaper than that.

What the sales did not provide for my horse to wear, I hoped that casual conversation might. So, like a man on a furtive hunt for contraband, I would take people aside and whisper, 'Do you know where there's any harness for sale?' It became an obsessive search that took me into places I might not otherwise have ventured – like the harness-maker's in the Suffolk village of Debenham. The front door of this high-street shop is split like a stable door, and by merely opening the top half you release the heady aroma of leather being worked. Open the bottom half of the door and step inside, and if the billy-stove is roaring away you can easily be intoxicated by the smell of hide and wax – with just a hint of horse on the saddles and bridles that are in for repair.

On the wall, in the bay window where the saddler sits with his commanding view of the main street, are pictures of horses at plough – the Clarks' horses, of course. He found me some odd bits to go in dutfins (bridles) and a wooden tree for a cart saddle, and he repaired collars I had brought home from sales, and patiently listened to my harness problems, expounded round the big black billy-stove. And like so many people I met in my quest to 'do right by Punch', the saddler listened with great patience and sympathy to the confused ramblings of a beginner.

One thing that was forcibly brought home to me was my lack of real knowledge. I had a considerable amount of experience, having tackled more or less every job on Weylands Farm, but by the time December came and the day grew ever nearer when Punch would be mine and have to come home with me, I grappled with my memory to try and dredge up just how certain jobs were done. Not complicated ones, but simple jobs like setting up harrows and harnessing a pair of horses to them. I had done it myself, and seen it done many times, but the prospect of doing it alone, at home, with Punch had me asking more detailed questions than had ever crossed my mind in the previous eleven months. Even the basics were beyond me, like the tying of the 'top latch' – a strip of leather a little thicker than a bootlace that drew together the two wooden hames that sat either side of the collar and through which the horse transmitted its pulling power. If the top latch gives, so does the whole harness, with disastrous consequences under some circumstances. For example, what if the horse were hauling a ton of mangels up a hill and the vital connection parted? These thoughts occupied much of my mind, and when I had the chance I nipped behind the feed store to the racks where the working harness was kept, and examined it in some detail.

My visits to Weylands Farm had become so much a regular part of life that it was difficult to believe they would soon come to an end. On 'farming days', as I called them, I would be up at six, and six sharp, for if it was any later I wouldn't be at the farm by seven and Cheryl was bound to remark. I would pack a few sandwiches for lunch, usually bread and cheese or ham with mustard, wrap them in paper and stuff them in a canvas bag I had bought in an army surplus shop specially for the purpose. In my early days I foolishly thought that a sandwich box would do the job, but a plastic box cannot be hung from the harness of a horse, and leading horses to a field with one hand while trying to hold the precious lunchbox in the other is no fun. So, like the old horsemen, I got the horse to carry the lunch for me. My wife tried to press on me yoghurts and fancy cheeses and other foods of the '80s, but they seemed out of place. I hadn't the heart to ask a Suffolk Punch to haul a Sainsbury's Individual Chocolate Mousse up and down a ploughed field, but hunks of bread and cheese I felt sure he wouldn't mind.

169

I often wondered if I would have liked to have done this job for real: to have been a horseman and to have been forced to work the land in exchange for a meagre living. I was always aware that I was in a privileged position where I could turn my back on the toil if I so wished, climb into my heated car after a hard day in the field and be certain of a hot bath and a good meal after a mucky day carting mangels.

Alongside my farming books grew a collection of books about farming life rather than just farming practice. I read tales of Victorian times when the farm work would not have differed much from life on Weylands Farm. One memorable passage from such a book was the story of a young girl.

> She had taken her clothes off and wrung them out and put them to dry on the top of the wheat. Often when it came on to rain there was no shelter within reach, but if there was any the gangmaster would not let us go till we were drenched. The man knocked us about and ill-used us dreadfully with hoes, spuds and everything, he would not care what.

A single example, but one which stuck in my mind when I walked the corn fields with the relaxed air of one who could afford to hit back, and say no.

But the farm-worker's life, with all its gruelling frustrations, still held a fascination for me after almost a year on the land. I wanted to know more, and by knowing and learning and showing genuine interest I hoped I could become in some small way one of them – because I respected them for the work they did and the lives they lived. My motives were not always fully understood, however. When I decided to have made for me a Suffolk suit, I felt the occasional sharp edge of a local tongue when someone felt that I had overstepped the mark.

The Suffolk suit came about after a conversation I had with our local plumber. He is called Bill Horne, and has a beard as long and as wild and as grey as Moses'. He is a folk musician and, being Suffolk born and bred and having played for long hours in pubs, he knows as much about tradition in the area in which he lives as any man. It was he who told me of the Suffolk suit: a three-piece suit of heavy tweed that farmers would have worn either for work or for Sunday best. It was a complete insulation system, being made out of cloth so thick that the trousers should stand of their own accord. I looked at some old farming photos and noticed how the Suffolk suit was carefully designed to accommodate an expanding girth. One simply did up fewer of the buttons the stouter one became. One picture in particular took my eye of a white-bearded old boy who had grown so vast round the waist that the only button that met was the one at the collar. I decided to have a Suffolk suit.

After a search which involved the local newspaper and a barrage of phone calls in response to my plea for a tailor, I found an old man of eighty-two, Bob Plant, who said he could show me how one was made; and a young local tailor called Tony Hawkins who said he would make one for me if he could. I brought the new brain and the old together and the result was a piece of art, in heavy Derby tweed, that would keep out any chill wind that a farming year could throw at me. The trousers were thick and mud-proof, cut high at the back to clad the loins, with a waistcoat cut low to allow no perilous gap between it and the trouser tops. The fly 'arrangements' were unusual in that instead of a row of buttons, the trousers had a broad flap which buttoned both sides, and dropped when required. These were called 'ready boys'. Shrouding the whole thing was an overcoat that buttoned high up to the neck. I loved it. Everyone on Weylands Farm loved it, and when a picture duly appeared in the local paper I had many calls of appreciation.

But there was one letter of cruel condemnation. 'Who did I think I was?' was its tone. 'Why should I be playing at Suffolk farm-workers?' And by implication, 'Why didn't I get back where I belonged on the TV?'

Now, if this had been a letter of criticism written after a TV show, it would have drained off this particular duck's back (especially if I had been wearing the impenetrable suit at the time), but it cut deep. I wanted to make them understand that I had done what I had done out of genuine interest in the working of the land. I did not, however, hesitate to wear the, by now, plough-stained suit when Weylands Farm held its Christmas dinner at the Bell Hotel in the Suffolk village of Kersey.

It was a formal occasion in many ways, with Roger saying grace before we sat down to dinner, but it was a joyful one too. This was an honest gathering of a dozen or so people who, in their individual ways, had safely brought Weylands Farm through another year. Stuart and Fred were there from the forge, and Busky was there too. The girls who cleaned harness for shows were there, and so was Tom Walne, the 'gang-leader' at thrashing time, and master mechanic too.

We tucked into hearty plates of beef and pork and Roger sent back some fancy mashed potato and insisted on chips. By the time the Christmas pudding was being offered round, the story-telling and the singing had begun. It was a simple but effective entertainment prompted by

Roger, who called, 'Are you going to sing for us, Sandy?', at which Sandy bravely got to her feet and sang gypsy and romantic songs. Then Tom told a story about his long, slow horse-drawn journey from Suffolk to Appleby horse fair in a traditional gypsy caravan. It was an evening of simplicity, of songs and story-telling, and harmless ribaldry. Roger especially liked to retell old battles of wills, and words. Like the case of one 'boy' who was sent by his father to Roger as an apprentice farrier. As Roger said with great gusto, 'After a few days, his father came to me and asked me what I made of him. I told him. I said, "If he'd been mine I'd have drowned him at birth and raised a pig on the milk!"'

Stories were always in the air at Weylands Farm and would suddenly emerge at the kitchen table, in the odd corner of a barn, or on social occasions like these. I can only recall a few, and hesitate to record them in case they are not exactly as told. But since stories get better with the hazy blur of hindsight, let me tell you some I particularly remember.

Claude, the retired wart-charmer (who, incidentally, once listed his professions in a Suffolk *Who's Who* as 'chimney-sweep and cat castrater' — he used to wrap the cats in a sack and put a wellington boot over their head; one particular cat, sensing the approach of Claude's knife, made a run for it through the kitchen window and when the owner called for it the next day, he told her it had 'died under the anaesthetic'), always told the story of the man in Boxford who had a lion which he led around on a chain. This man used to ride a 'wall of death' at Clacton with the lion on the handlebars.

It sounded very unlikely to me. However, Claude can take you to the spot in the garden of the White Hart in

Boxford where the lion reposes. That's true, that is, as Roger might say.

Roger used to recall his younger days when he lived in the Suffolk market town of Saxmundham.

'I was with an old boy who went to Saxmundham and bought a piano at the auction. We took it home in the horse and cart. Well, we got to the railway line and the gates were shut because a train was coming and in front of us was a Jaguar car. Well, the old boy got down from the cart, opened the door of the Jaguar and got in. "Do you want to buy a piano?" he said. "I can deliver it." '

I wonder if it was the same old boy who lived in a chicken hut and claimed that he was a Lord of the Land? Roger did explain how and why, but the finer details of these stories fade. Perhaps it was also the same man who Roger said 'never washed his porridge pan', so that as the years went by a thickening crust developed inside the pan and there was now just enough room to get a spoon inside, where once upon a time there had been a good twelve inches of space to stir around in.

If Weylands Farm ever chooses to have its own coat of arms 'Once upon a Time' would be a good motto.

My farming year came full circle as Roger announced one morning that we were to go to plough. 'I've got *your* pair going well,' he told me. My pair? 'Punch and Star, they're going real good together,' said Roger. We collared the horses; Roger was to plough with Thomas and Rupert, me with Punch and Star. I was just about to walk out to the yard, having watered the horses and checked the harness, when Roger cried 'Woah!' 'Head horseman allus go first,' he told me, and I stood aside to let him pass and humbly followed on behind. I felt flattered rather than

174

rebuked, because it was a sign that he was now thinking of me as a part of the farm and not a student to whom the rules did not fully apply. Of course, it was a sensible rule that all the others should follow the head horseman both on to and off the fields. It meant that the man in charge was dictating the hours of work and no one 'clocked off' till the boss did.

We ambled up the lane, turned left and plodded up the long muddy track to what we called the Pill Box field because it had a concrete relic of the Second World War slap in the middle of it. I led Punch, and Star followed on behind. Roger showed me how to fasten a line from the bearing rein of the leading horse to the hames of the one that was to follow. It was one of the many inspired devices of horse control I had seen, for the leading horse could always drag the one behind a little faster if need be; but if the slower one couldn't keep up, the tension on the bearing rein and thence the bit would increase and the leading horse would slow down a bit.

I kept a firm hold on Punch's leading rein, but Roger didn't bother holding his. He just strolled up the hill, and Thomas and Rupert followed like faithful dogs trailing their master.

Once on the field, Roger hitched his horses to the waiting plough and I swung mine into position so that they were standing side by side and just in front of their pair of wooden whippletrees to which the hooks on their pulling chains would attach. I tied a length of line between their two mouths and carefully knotted the ends on to the bits in such a way that it could easily be pulled undone in the event of a disaster. Then I tied the plough line, one end to the outside of each horse's bit, and led it backwards to the plough. This would be my steering line, or rein. Then I took the hooks which were resting on a ring on the harness, led them back to the whippletrees and carefully hooked them on, the hooked end pointing to the inside so as not to catch on posts or trees. When both sides had been done, my two horses were ready to go to plough. I felt proud, expert. Roger came striding over.

'Hang on, mate! You've got 'em the wrong way round. You want Punch as your furrow horse 'cos he walks straight. Swap them old devils round.' And so I unhooked all that I had hooked, untied all that I had carefully knotted and, with the horses swapped round, I started again.

When all was ready I took hold of the wooden handles of the plough and looked at Roger, who was already under way and scything his way through the earth.

We were not starting on a new field, we were finishing off what little remained after several days' hard work by others, and I glanced at the perfect way in which strips of earth had been rolled over on to each other by whoever had ploughed the stetches I was to finish off. There was not one blemish I could see in the work that had already been done; no lack of precision, no errors which would betray a slackness in the work of either the horses or the men.

I did not have to make much adjustment to the plough myself, thank God. It was the same plough that had been used by the previous toiler. It was a question of simply switching on and going, and so I bore down on the plough handles and called to Punch and Star 'Gee . . . urp!' They heaved themselves forward, slowly and reluctantly at first, but I gave them a more clipped 'G'up' and they were away. Punch settled into his furrow and plodded as carefully as a man painting white lines down the middle of the road. Star, in his less intelligent but equally willing way, was plodding nice and steadily the landward side.

As soon as we picked up speed, the plough bit and started its work of turning the earth, of wiping out all memory of the previous agricultural year and getting ready for the new. All errors, all tragedies of the previous farming year would be hidden and forgotten as the plough sped on, raising new hope from the old soil below. It didn't matter any longer that this was the field where the binder had magically cut the rye and the monstrous thrashing machine had beaten the precious grain from those carefully 'stooked' sheaves. It just didn't matter any more. The only thought was of the future, of finishing the ploughing, of harrowing, drilling and rolling and, with luck, a better year to come.

'Whoo . . . ah,' I called as we came to the end of the furrow. The horses stood for a minute and reached out with their teeth to try and grab a bit of succulence from a twig of a tree. But they weren't quite close enough. Perhaps next time. 'Cup, cup, old hoss,' I called and they hardly moved a step. 'PUNCH!' I bellowed, and with a guiding tug on the left rein he started to bear to the left, pushing Star, who seemed to have dropped into a deep sleep in the few moments he had been standing still on the headland.

'Cup, cup,' I called again, using the words that Roger and Cheryl use to guide and steer their horses. 'Cup' is the order to turn to the left. It is an abbreviation of 'cup'we', which in turn is a shortening of 'come to me'. As horses are always led from the nearside, 'come to me' means turn to where you find me.

177

The word for a turn to the right is more difficult to explain. The word itself seems to vary from Roger to Cheryl to Gerry, but is usually either 'weetch' or 'weesh'. I can offer no explanation. 'Go back' is another vital order at which the horse will ease back a step or two, and usually appears on the lips as 'Ho-bak!' So, as you turn the plough at the end of the furrow it is a combination of 'Cup cup cup, old hoss . . . whoah . . . ho-bak . . . woah . . . cup, juss one step. . . .'

'Keep talking to your hosses,' Roger always told me, and so after a few conversations such as I have described, I was able to position the plough at the beginning of what was to be the next furrow without too much heaving and manhandling of the plough. Ploughs are heavy things and meant to be hauled by horses, not men. Of course, I didn't always get it in the right spot and then I had to jiggle it about myself, which was arm-wrenching work.

'Get your hosses lined up so that when they set off they're heading where you want 'em to go. Don't have to jiggle with them when you've set off.'

I called, 'G'up,' and we set off back up the field to cut the second furrow. It was just a year since I had cut my first furrow, and although I had done none of it since, I found the feel of the plough strangely familiar. I was beginning to sense when the plough would need guiding or when I would have to bear down to dig deeper if we happened upon a harder patch.

'You see that bit up there,' Roger said, pointing to two tramline-like undulations that were clearly visible on the surface of the freshly ploughed field. 'That was where someone ran a tractor over here during the summer. Now, that compressed that land so much that even when it's ploughed you can still see where it'd bin. That'il take

178

years to plough that out, y'know. Years!' It was only the repeated passing of the tractor that had compacted the soil and made it hard and unyielding. By comparison, the land around it where only the horses had trodden was crumbly and friable. Land that is regularly under the machine gets more and more dense, and increasingly powerful engines are needed to work it. The coming of the tractor meant that respect for the soil moved lower down the list of a farmer's priorities.

I called to my horses and off we set again, but this time less steadily and not with as much order as before. The plough wavered and meandered and I could feel trembling through the wooden handles.

'Stun!' shouted Roger. I begged his pardon. 'You've got a stun stuck in it.' I kicked the earth away from between the coulter and the tip of the plough-share, and there was a mighty flint firmly lodged between them. I knocked it out with the rusty spanner that was always hanging from the shafts of the plough and we set off again. Soon we were at the headland again; I turned the horses, trying hard to get the plough into the perfect starting position without having to carry any of its weight myself. But this calls for precision halting of the horses on the headland and turning back towards the field at exactly the right moment. Although this time was better than the last, it was not accurate enough and I had a good deal of humping and heaving to do.

'G'up,' and we were away again. Roger was heading towards us. I cannot say why or how, but in an instant the plough jumped out of the ground and the horses, seemingly out of control, dragged it aimlessly across the field. I dropped the plough handles and grabbed the plough line. 'WOOOAH . . . WOOAH!' I cried with a hint of desperation as the horses broke into a confused trot. I pulled with little effect, and shouted, but only after they had thundered a good fifty yards did they eventually stop.

Roger halted his horses and strolled over. 'You want to be a bit gentle in your voice, talk to them more. You've got to sing to them . . . whoo . . . ooo.'

He picked up the plough lines, turned the horses full circle and brought the plough back to the place where the upset had first begun. 'They know they've done wrong. They know it.'

I called to them and we headed on down the rest of the furrow as though nothing had happened. I knew now where those wretched tractor marks were and was ready for them; if they caught you unawares they could easily throw your plough out of the furrow. Being a typical beginner, I was fine as long as all was going well but uncertain when faced with a major problem.

'You're having the best of it, and the worst of it,' chuckled Roger as we passed – me heading up the field, and he in the other direction, following me and correcting any waviness in my work. 'That's not a bad furrow, not bad at all,' he would say to encourage me, and if I was not getting the results, he was soon over to show me why.

The light was fading now. The church tower at Stoke-by-Nayland had been brilliantly lit by the low and mellow winter sun; but the sun had gone and taken with it all sight of the church. The stillness of the cool afternoon had given way to a gentle breeze that brought a shiver with it and a mist that hung over the fields and poured down the valleys to smother the village. Soon we would be turning into the furrow for the last time, unhooking the horses and walking them home for a rich and well earned feed of bran, oats and chaff, and all the other grains that these benign monsters help to grow and love to devour.

As we walked down the lane, I hoped we might see sparks rise from their feet as their huge steel shoes hit the flints. I had read of it, but longed to see it. There was still so much that I wanted to see, and learn, and do, but I had set myself to work as a farmer's boy for a year and my year was at its end.

I glanced round to see if Roger had finished yet, but I saw that he was still bent over his plough, still calling to his horses. So I turned the plough and with a 'G'up' we marched on yet again. We threw the earth aside and turned the old soil into new, and as I walked the furrow I thought how nothing could eradicate from my mind the memory of this glorious, fulfilling and inspiring year. Nothing could ever have the force to plough across my memories of Weylands Farm, of Roger and Cheryl Clark and their Suffolk horses.

I pressed harder on the plough handles, so deep in thought that I almost missed those damned tractor ruts. I thought how Gerry would have cursed. I thought of the horses, the Suffolk Punches, and how generous they had been to this humble beginner. They could have made a fool of me if they had wished. Surely they sensed that this particular farmer's boy knew less than most. I shall miss them, and the laughter round the kitchen table. I shall miss the good honest labour as well: the drudgery on the wet, cold days on the chilly, sodden soil or in the muddy yard where the only relief from the aching and stinking muck-carting was the prospect of a cup of mid-morning tea passed through the kitchen window. I decided that I must be amongst the luckiest men on earth to have been allowed, for a year, to be part of the magic that is performed every day of every farming year at Weylands Farm.

'Wooah . . .' I called, and the horses came to a smart halt, just close enough this time to grab a mouthful of juicy twig. I turned them and looked along the furrow I had just cut. It was darker now, and mistier, but I could see its straightness stretching into the distance. Hadn't Roger told me that a good furrow was one you could see a mouse running along? I called him over for his judgement.

'Roger,' I shouted, but there was no reply. I looked around but the mist had thickened and I could see no sign of him; in the rising whistle of the wind, my voice must have been lost.

So I stood, for the last time, with my horses and my plough and took one final lingering look at that furrow, till the mist took it from me.

# Postscript

THE following Sunday, the huge and impressive lorry that proudly bears the name 'R.J. & C.J. CLARK' drew up outside our house. The ramp was dropped and down it marched two shining and fit Suffolk Punches. One was called Punch, and not surprisingly the other was called Star. I had always wanted Punch, and now he was mine; but Star couldn't be left without him, not after seven years of working together. Who would have the heart to split such a team?

Roger offered me a few bits of machinery that he had no further use for, which I added to the pieces I had eagerly collected at my beloved farm sales, and shortly we shall get to work. What we shall do is far from certain. I hope, at least, that they will help to grow most of their own food. But as one old Suffolk horseman said to me when asked why he still kept his old hoss, ' 'Cos I just likes him to talk to.' Punch, Star and I have a lot to tell each other.

# APPENDIX 1

One summer's afternoon, Roger happened to call on Claude, the old wart-charmer. He lived in a single-storey cottage at the bottom of the hill that led to Weylands Farm, alongside the river and close to the old water mill. Here, Claude kept farm hours although long-since retired. At seven o'clock in the morning, which was the time I was usually driving past, I would see a cloud of black smoke coming from his chimney. Claude liked to be up and about.

But like many people I have met in Suffolk of his generation, they do not readily give a lot away. They are often generous to a fault with their accumulated wisdom, but if you don't bother to ask a question they will not volunteer any information. I have struggled for hours with a bit of fencing while an old boy leaned on the gate and silently looked on. After I had struggled for at least an hour to make a decent job, and failed, he would then and only then say, 'I c'd a tol'd yer yer weren't startin' that job right!'

That was how Claude managed for many years to confine to himself the names of the fields that make up Weylands Farm. Field names are a great tradition, and many are now lost for ever as hedges are removed and 'Horse Meadow', for example, is joined to 'Apple Field' and the new farmer can't think of anything more imaginative to call it than 'Twenty-Acre Field'.

Learning the traditional names of the fields at Weylands Farm was, for Roger, not unlike discovering a family tree. On a scrap of map which Claude had harboured in an old plastic bag were the roots of the farm. Roger happened to come across this just as Claude was thinking of throwing it out.

With the help of Roger's personal records kept in a dog-eared notebook, I have recorded the entire farming activity on Weylands Farm for 1987.

### The Fields

| | | |
|---|---|---|
| Bush Field | 12 acres | winter barley (contracted out) |
| Stable Field | 2 acres | potatoes |
| | 2 acres | kale |
| Rail Lands | 3 acres | spring barley |
| | 2 acres | kale |
| | 1 acre | meadow |
| Wet Field | 2 acres | mangels |
| | 1 acre | oats/tares (fed off, ploughed early and sown with rye for early feeding of lambs) |
| | 1 acre | lucerne |
| | 1 acre | kale (late sown) |
| Ram's Field | 11 acres | winter barley |
| Cock's Hill | 8 acres | grass |
| Porter's Field | 5 acres | winter barley undersown with grass |
| Gages | 15 acres | spring beans |
| Little Bromehill | 8 acres | spring oats undersown with red clover to make 'stover' (clover hay – very good feed for Suffolk horses) |
| Great Bromehill | 13 acres | rye undersown with turnips |
| Betty Groves | 10 acres | wheat (crop failed) |
| Cross (Pill Box) Field | 8 acres | rye undersown with turnips |
| Wheeping Hills | 8 acres | spring barley undersown with turnips |
| Post Office Field | 5 acres | wheat (poor crop) |

### The Farm Animals

Number of horses in work: 6

Prince, Rupert, Thomas, Toby, Richard and Courtier (Courtier was found dead in his stable one morning in late December. It was a sudden and painless death as there was no evidence of kicking and no sounds had been heard.)

2 hunters

('That's our relaxation in the winter,' said Roger, 'hunting with the Essex and Suffolk Foxhounds.')

20 pedigree ewes and followers

25 store lambs

260 sheep in to be fed

Cattle:

4 Red Poll
1 Angus/Friesian
15 followers and store cattle

Horses shod:

2508 sets of shoes

25 colts of various breeds broken to harness for customers

2 ferrets

2 collies (Fern and Meg)

2 terriers (Sally and Fred)

9 geese

5 ducks

numerous hound puppies 'at walk' (being schooled for the hunting field)

various chickens

1 fat black and white cat (I asked the name and after a blank look or two passed between Roger and Cheryl, assuming it to be a recent acquisition, I asked how long it had been on the farm. 'Sixteen years,' I was told.)

# APPENDIX 2

If the Clarks were in the racehorse business and were as successful at winning races as they are at winning prizes at county shows with their Suffolks, they and their horses would be worth millions. However, as Roger once told me, 'The true value of any horse is what you get for him on the butcher's hook. Any money above that is a bonus.'

However, that cannot detract from a glorious year with as many first prizes as anyone could wish for. They are recorded below in the order in which they took place.

Newark and Notts Show
    3rd in single and pairs class with Thomas and Richard in a class for all breeds of heavy horse

Woodbridge Horse Show (a main event for Suffolk horses)
    Thomas: champion gelding
    Richard: reserve champion gelding
    Thomas: reserve supreme champion
    Thomas: horse with best feet
    Thomas: best single turnout
    Richard: 2nd in decorated horse class

South Suffolk Show
    Thomas: supreme champion
    Richard: 2nd in gelding class
    1st prize for pen of ewes and lambs

Hadleigh Show
    Thomas: champion Suffolk Horse
    Thomas: 2nd in best feet class
    Sheep:    3rd prize Suffolk ram
              2nd prize for pen of ewes and lambs

Hertford Show (heavy horses of any breed)
    Richard: 3rd in single turnout

Richard/Thomas: 1st pairs of heavy horses (any breed!)
            champion turnout of all single, pairs and teams
            ('A remarkable feat!' says Cheryl)
Thomas: reserve champion heavy horse of the show

Suffolk Show
   Richard: champion gelding
   Thomas: reserve champion gelding
          cup for the best two Suffolk horses
   Thomas: Suffolk horse with the best feet
          1st in teams of heavy horses of any breed ('Beating
          the Shires!' says Roger)
          4th in pairs
          4th in single turnout
   Roger Clark was judged National Suffolk Punch Shoeing
   Champion and Best Local Contestant (Shoeing)
   The 'boy' Fred won the apprentice class
   Red Poll cow: 4th dry cow class

Royal Cornwall Show
   Richard: best heavy horse in show
          best agricultural working horse

South of England Show
   Richard: best agricultural horse of any breed
          1st in single turnout

Royal Norfolk Show
   Thomas: 1st in class and reserve champion overall
   Richard: 2nd in class
          1st in class for single, pairs or teams of any breed

Royal Show
   Richard:
   Thomas: 2nd in class
          1st in single, pair and team class for Suffolk horses

Tendring Show
   Richard: champion Suffolk horse
          supreme champion heavy horse overall

Thomas: reserve champion Suffolk horse
          2nd in pairs
          2nd in class for pen of ewe lambs

Royal Welsh
  3rd in single and pairs

Royal Yorkshire
  Richard/Thomas: 2nd in single turnout
                  2nd in pairs turnout (against 25 other turn-
                  outs of all breeds)

# APPENDIX 3

Anyone wishing to know more about the Suffolk horse and East Anglian life and farming methods can do no better than study the writings of George Ewart Evans. Although born a Welshman, he developed a deep love for East Anglia, and his book *The Horse in the Furrow* is the finest record there is of the history of the Suffolk horse and horsemen. In his other books, based largely on conversations he recorded whilst travelling with his tape-recorder, including *Ask the Fellows Who Cut the Hay*, *The Pattern Under the Plough*, *The Farm and the Village* and *Horse Power and Magic*, he provides a vivid record of East Anglian life in the days when all farms were like Weylands Farm.

In some of his books he writes admiringly of Roger and Cheryl Clark and he sadly died during the writing of this book.

For a record of a farming year in the heyday of the Suffolk horse, I must also mention *Early to Rise: A Suffolk Morning* by Hugh Barrett, a real 'farmer's boy'. This gem of a book has now been republished in paperback by the Farming Press and fans of it need no longer engage in dusty searches through second-hand book-shops.

Since leaving Weylands Farm, I have continued to work Suffolk Punches on my own small farm and I have recorded my adventures every Saturday in *The Times*. Two collections of these columns have now been published: *Farming Times* and *Second Crop* (both published by Victor Gollancz).

If you have read the book and now 'want to see the movie', I can recommend a video which Roger, Cheryl and I made in 1993 called 'Harnessed to the Plough'. It follows a year on Weylands Farm and can be enjoyed by lovers of horses, traditional farming enthusiasts and anyone who simply wants to sit back and enjoy the views (Farming Press £14.95).

Finally, the Suffolk Horse Society holds through its members a treasure chest of knowledge and wisdom. Membership is open to all who have an interest in the Suffolk horse, and not owning one does not in any way prevent you from joining. Apart from their work in supporting the breed at county and agricultural shows, the society holds social evenings. These are jovial occasions, and sometimes unpredictable. I remember one where alongside the usual raffle prizes of the bottle of sherry and the box of chocolates appeared a fine leg of pork. I remember Roger leaning over to me and whispering, 'Someone will have had a pig die this morning!'

Horse-owning members are enthusiastic and helpful to new-comers, as I have found. Many of the more senior members will have forgotten more about horsemanship than most of us will ever know. The enthusiastic secretary, Philip Ryder-Davies, will ensure that you get a warm welcome. The Suffolk Horse Society address is Market Hill, Woodbridge, Suffolk.

In 1994, after an intensive fund-raising campaign, the Suffolk Horse Society opened a museum in Woodbridge. The Suffolk horse is now the only breed of heavy horse to have a museum which charts its history. The museum depicts the farming year, the lives of the horsemen, farriers, blacksmith and harness-makers who were part of the rural scene at the time the Suffolk Punch worked the farmland of East Anglia. The museum is open every afternoon from 2–5 pm and I guarantee you will spend an enjoyable afternoon soaking up the history of this magnificent breed of carthorse.

# Farming Press Books & Videos

Below is a sample of the wide range of agricultural and veterinary books and videos published by Farming Press. For more information or for a free illustrated catalogue of all our publications please contact:

**Farming Press Books & Videos, Wharfedale Road**
**Ipswich IP1 4LG, United Kingdom**
**Telephone (0473) 241122    Fax (0473) 240501**

### Harnessed to the Plough (VHS VIDEO)
**Roger & Cheryl Clark with Paul Heiney**

Roger and Cheryl Clark demonstrate a year of contemporary horse-drawn cultivations and harvesting on their Suffolk farm. Additional commentary by Paul Heiney.

### Early to Rise
**Hugh Barrett**

An authentic and highly praised account of life as a farm pupil in the early 1930s.

### The Hired Lad
**Ian Thomson**

A young man's first work on a Scottish farm when horses were yielding to tractor and bothy life was rough and ready.

### The Horse in Husbandry
**Jonathan Brown**

Photographs of horses working on farms from 1890 to 1950, with an account of how they were managed.

### Farming Through the Ages
**Robert Trow-Smith**

From earliest times to World War II, an account of Britain's farming history built around a remarkable collection of pictures.

### The Spacious Days
**Michael Twist**

Growing up on a Buckinghamshire estate in the 1930s. Anecdotes about the farm staff, agricultural work, gamekeeping and the countryside.

Farming Press Books & Videos is part of the Morgan-Grampian Farming Press Group which publishes a range of farming magazines: *Arable Farming*, *Dairy Farmer*, *Farming News*, *Pig Farming*, *What's New in Farming*. For a specimen copy of any of these please contact the address above.